Unlocking the Potential of Post-Industrial Cities

UNLOCKING THE POTENTIAL OF POST-INDUSTRIAL CITIES

Matthew E. Kahn and Mac McComas

JOHNS HOPKINS UNIVERSITY PRESS BALTIMORE

Printed in the United States of America on acid-free paper
9 8 7 6 5 4 3 2 1

Johns Hopkins University Press
2715 North Charles Street
Baltimore, Maryland 21218-4363
www.press.jhu.edu

Library of Congress Cataloging-in-Publication Data

Names: Kahn, Matthew E., 1966– author. | McComas, Mac, 1988– author.
Title: Unlocking the potential of post-industrial cities / Matthew E. Kahn and Mac McComas.
Description: Baltimore : Johns Hopkins University Press, 2021. | Includes bibliographical references and index.
Identifiers: LCCN 2020036272 | ISBN 9781421440828 (paperback) | ISBN 9781421440835 (ebook)
Subjects: LCSH: Urban renewal—United States—Case studies. | City planning—United States—Case studies. | Community development, Urban—United States—Economic aspects—Case studies. | Community development, Urban—United States—Social aspects—Case studies. | Labor supply—United States—Case studies.
Classification: LCC HT175 .K34 2021 | DDC 307.3/4160973—dc23
LC record available at https://lccn.loc.gov/2020036272

A catalog record for this book is available from the British Library.

Special discounts are available for bulk purchases of this book. For more information, please contact Special Sales at specialsales@jh.edu.

Johns Hopkins University Press uses environmentally friendly book materials, including recycled text paper that is composed of at least 30 percent post-consumer waste, whenever possible.

Contents

Preface

Over centuries, America's older center cities have experienced growth in population and prosperity, but in recent decades, some of them have experienced decline. At any point in time, a city's history influences the look and feel of the city's built environment of houses, businesses, green spaces, and other physical infrastructure. Memories of this history affect personal interactions between groups. While history matters, expectations about the future of the place are crucial in influencing events of the present.

This book studies this interplay between history and expectations in determining the quality of life and economic growth dynamics of six major US cities. Although we approach this topic from the perspective of microeconomics, our study is informed by interdisciplinary interactions with our colleagues.

At Johns Hopkins University, the 21st Century Cities Initiative is a cross-campus urban research center that brings together faculty and researchers from the Krieger School of Arts & Sciences, the Bloomberg School of Public Health, the Whiting School of Engineering, the Carey School of Business, the School of Medicine, the School of Education, the School of Advanced International Studies, and the School of Nursing. What unites us is our common interest in how to translate research ideas into improving urban quality of life.

We must acknowledge some people whose insights have greatly improved this book. These include two anonymous reviewers, Matthew McAdam, Robert Brown, Steve Olson, Carol Kahn, Nancy McDonald, Beth Blauer, Vrshank Ravi, Kylie Patterson, Ben Seigel, Michael Braverman, Mary Miller, Andrew Cherlin, Deborah Gross, Lindsay Thompson, Stefanie DeLuca, Robert Lieberman, Jeff Lin, Randy Walsh, Marc Votruba, Pete Saunders, Phil Leaf, Steve Tobocman, Robert Embry, and Nolan Jones.

Unlocking the Potential of Post-Industrial Cities

1

Cities at a Crossroads

Cities can be exciting and dynamic places. When people, goods, and ideas move within a small geographic area, transportation is less costly, and learning and trade are facilitated. Well-paid people living close together can create enough demand to support cultural and religious institutions, a variety of shops and restaurants, and professional sports teams. When the local economy is flourishing, tax revenues are high enough that local governments can implement policies to improve the quality of life and help their residents escape poverty.

Cities also have their downsides. In the early 20th century, US cities suffered from infectious disease outbreaks associated with dirty water. In 2020, the spread of the coronavirus across US cities highlighted one of the demons of density. Even during normal times, living and working at high density imposes costs. People in cities are more likely to be exposed to crime, pollution, and traffic. This book focuses on the challenges for the center city of a metropolitan area. We define a center city as the central urban political jurisdiction in a metropolitan area, such as that of the City of Philadelphia. Most center cities, viewed apart from their surrounding suburbs, have pockets of concentrated poverty where many people live in conditions that make it difficult for them to achieve their goals and for their children to achieve their full potential.

Over time, some cities become stronger while others grow weaker. Between 1970 and 2018, the population of the City of Las Vegas grew from 126,000 to 644,000; during those same years, Baltimore City's population shrank from 906,000 to 603,000. Cities also differ with respect to their population's skill level and poverty rate. In 2010, relative to the national urban average, Baltimore residents were less likely to be college graduates and more likely to be living in poverty.

This book explores why six center cities stretching from the mid-Atlantic states to the central Midwest—Baltimore, Cleveland, Detroit, Philadelphia, Pittsburgh, and St. Louis—have lost population and seen their poverty rates rise over the past 50 years. More than 3.8 million people live in these cities. More than a quarter of their residents are poor, and more than half are African American. Why aren't more people in these cities enjoying the American Dream of upward mobility? Why haven't more companies moved to these cities or started up in them? Why have politicians, business interests, and community leaders been unsuccessful in rebuilding these cities after major industries left?

Our six cities are not homogenous; some have enjoyed greater success in fostering economic development, reducing violent crime, educating the next generation, and ameliorating poverty. Philadelphia and Pittsburgh, among our set of six, have experienced the most progress, as synergies between their universities and medical centers have caused growth in high-tech jobs. Our six cities may not be the same, but they do have similar histories and a common set of challenges that we highlight throughout the book. They also offer case studies of places where people struggle to achieve the American Dream. The lessons learned from them can be applied to struggling neighborhoods in cities across America with high levels of violent crime, stagnant job growth, low educational attainment, and environmental challenges.

Our six cities are often portrayed as dangerous, dirty, poor, and corrupt shells of their former industrial glory. This coarse description simultaneously borders on caricature and contains elements of truth. What is the urban experience for the millions of people who call these cities home? What differences exist among the neighborhoods that compose these cities? Millions of people watched HBO's show *The Wire*, which began by focusing on young men's drug-dealing activity in the poorest neighborhoods in Baltimore. What led men like those depicted in the show to their condition? What could improve their life outcomes and those of others in similarly dire situations?

The United States has more than 300 metropolitan areas in which people can live and work. Firms and people alike can "vote with their feet" as they seek out the place that is best for them. "Old cities" like the ones we analyze in this book have to compete to attract and retain people and employers in a post-industrial economy. In recent years, many people left cold cities of the Northeast for warmer Sunbelt cities. Because of this, our cities have to work extra hard to retain and attract residents. Even thriving cities like New York and Boston face the challenge of weather-induced out-migration.

The cities we study are at a crossroads. Depending on choices made today, these cities could enjoy a significant comeback, stagnate, or continue to decline. In cities enjoying a comeback, incumbent firms (i.e., established local companies with a proven market share) expand and hire local people to work. National firms locate branches in the city. Educated residents stay in the city, and migrants from outside the city move there. More people work and pay taxes. As local government elections become more competitive, politicians become more accountable to their constituents.

A major cause of the challenges these cities face is underinvestment. A four-dimensional coordination failure emerges. Cities do not invest enough in struggling neighborhoods. Young people do not invest enough in skill formation. Private real estate developers and businesses invest too little in projects that would create new local jobs. Banks and other financial institutions do not deploy enough capital and invest it in people and firms. These four sets of decisions are not made in isolation of each other; rather, they are interrelated and compounding. A type of catch-22 emerges. Young people foresee a bleak future in these cities without meaningful career paths. Thus, they underinvest in their skills. Firms are confronted with crime and poverty and a local workforce lacking the skills for 21st-century jobs. This pushes many firms into the suburbs and stunts the growth of the firms that remain. Cities that have a declining population with quality-of-life challenges and a weak local economy will have low real estate prices. This limits the ability of a city's elected leaders to make significant investments in costly education programs and to upgrade the city's aging transportation and other infrastructure.

Poor people who live in these cities do not want to be poor. In cities with economic growth but little upward mobility for the poor, rents will rise, thus displacing poor families to other areas. Ideally, local economic growth will create new jobs for local residents and an increase in the tax base that governments can use to expand social assistance programs and policies. The fate of urban people versus urban places hinges on whether the urban poor gain when neighborhoods gentrify. If they do not, they have less hope and less of a stake in supporting efforts for their city to make a comeback.

At a time of great social concern about economic inequality, some people voice a belief that our economy is a zero-sum game such that the wealthy gain from taking resources from the less fortunate. We embrace an alternative, more optimistic vision. In modern urban economies based on human capital (people's skills and personality traits), all people and communities can gain from investments in human capital.

The Urban Economics Approach

Drawing from the field of urban economics, our analysis stresses the central role of human capital in determining the productivity of individuals. We emphasize how important it is for cities to have the capacity to help young people build their skills and to retain and attract skilled people. We pay close attention to the challenges of crime and pollution that cities face. Safe, green cities represent a proven strategy of urban economic development, a strategy that the six cities profiled in this book could pursue.

People and firms have a choice of where they locate, and they will choose to live or locate in a place only if it currently outperforms, and is expected to in the future, their next best alternative. When better alternatives exist, people and firms will seek them out instead. Cities that do not offer high quality of life and amenities will lose people and firms to rival locations. Urban economics teaches us that wages and rents across cities will adjust over time to reflect the realities of supply and demand. If a city has an excess supply of vacant housing (because it was built decades ago when the city was booming) and a paucity of jobs, then both local real estate prices and wages will be low.

An urban economics approach to studying the causes and consequences of poor people living in poor places has a dual focus: diagnosing why this social challenge has arisen and suggesting politically palatable strategies to help poor people seeking employment, employers seeking to grow their businesses, and real estate interests seeking new opportunities. This emphasis on "growing the urban pie" rather than making moral arguments for redistributing a fixed pie (the zero-sum game) may frustrate some. While the Robin Hood approach to reducing income inequality is on some level just, economic logic demands that a city's mayor recognize that his or her actions will have intended and unintended consequences for which firms and people voluntarily locate within the city's boundaries. The six cities we study are large enough to be important for millions of people, but they are too small to determine the nation's overall "rules of the urban game." If Baltimore features high taxes and low quality of life, fewer people will choose to live there. Other areas may choose to have lower taxes or invest heavily in quality-of-life amenities as a competitive strategy to attract the well-to-do.

We do not know the exact recipe for success in our six cities. However, we offer a path forward for how these cities—and *all* cities—can identify policies and investments that reduce poverty and create shared prosperity. The work of the urban economist must be that of the humble doctor. We may not know the answer, but if we are able to craft a constructive path forward for diagnosing urban ills and designing and implementing solutions, we can foster progress while anticipating and mitigating the unintended consequences of well-meaning policies. In this book we propose a science-based approach that advocates a rigorous testing of policies and a scaling up of those policies that prove to be cost effective. Such experimentation creates a knowledge base about what works and why.

Economic and Demographic Trends

From 1950 to 2010, the population of the United States nearly doubled in a time of robust economic growth. Over this same period, the cities we study lost population and declined economically. How and why did that happen? Chapter two seeks an answer by looking at key demographic trends over time and across our six cities.

In the middle of the 20th century, each of our six cities featured a robust manufacturing sector, with Detroit and Pittsburgh being the most prominent. In 1950, the steel mill at Sparrows Point in Baltimore County provided more than 30,000 people with good jobs. Then the rise of international competition and the US South as a region of major production contributed to the decline of Rust Belt manufacturing. In 2012, the Sparrows Point steel mill went bankrupt and laid off its remaining 2,000 employees.

The closing of major firms in these cities had ripple effects on the local economy. Unemployment rates rose, and tax revenue declined. As the factories closed, the demand for the products offered by nearby suppliers plummeted. This created a second round of job losses, which further dragged down the local economy. Local stores and restaurants that had sold goods to people who lost their jobs faced lower demand.

The closing of factories with their high-wage manufacturing jobs had especially dire consequences for the African American community, although of course other groups were affected as well. People who had developed roots in these cities and had invested in skills tailored to their specific jobs could not easily get up and move. The homes in which they had invested earnings proceeded to lose their value after area job loss, suburbanization, blockbusting, and white flight had driven down the local demand for housing. But the housing itself was durable and rents had become cheap, so poor people stayed and the poverty challenge worsened.

Working-age men who lost their jobs also lost self-esteem and became more prone to substance abuse and encountered challenges at home. When their working skills atrophied, they became less likely to find a new job and less desirable as a husband. As marriage rates declined, female-headed households increased, and children had less contact with their father. The War on Drugs increased incarceration rates for minor nonviolent offenses, which disproportionately affected African American men.

The defunct factories left behind a legacy of polluted air, water, and soil. Poor people tend to live in the oldest and most polluted parts of cities and are exposed to higher levels of lead, airborne particulates, and other pollutants. Exposure to pollution exacerbates health and psychological problems. The result is disinvested people in disinvested neighborhoods with a toxic legacy, which helps create a cycle of poverty that is difficult to break.

The Demand for Labor

The most important market in any city is the labor market, since the job a person has usually determines that person's income. While those with access to cars can commute relatively easily around a city, this mode of transportation is expensive. Poor people usually depend on slow and unreliable public transit, and this limits their ability to access suburban jobs. Chapter three examines companies that are hiring and providing living-wage jobs in our six post-industrial cities.

Each city has an ecosystem of smaller firms that create job opportunities and the potential for growth. Each city also has a large enough population to create demand for a range of non-tradable services that can only be supplied locally, such as by doctor's offices, restaurants, car repair shops, and lawyer's offices. In recent decades, all our cities saw gains in employment in health care and social assistance industries, which is no surprise in cities such as Baltimore with Johns Hopkins Hospital and Cleveland with the Cleveland Clinic. In each of the cities, nonprofit entities such as the city government and local universities and hospitals employ large numbers of people. Many of these occupations are in education, safety, nursing, social work, and sanitation.

Each of the six cities was once a thriving manufacturing center that flourished because of its physical location. Geographic advantages—such as proximity to water and to consumer markets via existing railways, highways, and airports—still give them a cost advantage in receiving inputs to production and in shipping outputs to market.

The Supply of Labor

Given that many adults in the six cities do not own valuable assets, their annual income hinges on how many hours they work, their hourly wage, and any government transfers they receive. Who will have incomes above and below the poverty line? That depends, as chapter four explains, not only on whether jobs are available but on whether people are able to work at well-paying ones.

People with more education, more experience, and a higher level of skills that are in demand generally earn more. Relative to the nation as a whole, the workforce in our six cities lacks human capital. Both the urban young and middle-aged face many challenges that reduce their ability to participate in meaningful work, ranging from transportation to occupational licensing to criminal records to substance abuse to childcare to education.

Adults are less likely to be poor if they can look for work in a thriving local labor market. Teenagers are more likely to learn in school if they believe that they will find meaningful career paths once they graduate from high school. Young people are less likely to engage in unhealthy or criminal activities if they think they will have long lives and rewarding careers. In our six cities, the pathways to rewarding careers are not always apparent or easy to pursue. The odds are stacked against the cities' poor residents.

The Quality of Life in Urban Neighborhoods

Every city has some neighborhoods with a lower quality of life and others with a higher quality of life. Chapter five looks at the relationships among housing, quality of life, and where rich and poor people choose to live within metropolitan areas.

The real estate stock in our six cities is durable and was built for a larger population. As a result, each city has an excess supply of old and depreciating housing, which means that rents are very low in many parts of these cities. Abandoned buildings scar the local landscape and create areas ripe for drug dealing and disinvestment. Since rents are lower in neighborhoods with a lower quality of life, poor people tend to live there for extended periods. Lead levels are high in areas with older housing stock, contributing to both crime and poverty, which further compounds economic and social immobility.

In the cities we study, issues of poverty and race are closely connected. Our six cities feature a larger share of African Americans than the nation as a whole. The legacy of redlining, neighborhood racial covenants, and blockbusting persists in the spatial concentration and physical isolation of poor Blacks in high-poverty urban areas.

Regardless of race or ethnicity, concentrated urban poverty poses challenges for all residents of these areas. Residents in high-poverty areas face high crime rates and have poor-performing public schools. Richer people who live in our six cities face higher taxes to pay for programs aimed at mitigating the challenges faced by the urban poor. A low quality of life—along with a perception among outsiders that the quality of life is low—discourages outsiders from moving to an area. Retailers and restaurants tend not to open in these neighborhoods because they do not believe they can make a profit.

No flourishing American city has a major problem with violent crime. Given the media's focus on homicides, a high murder rate affects a city's reputation in the form of annual rankings of quality of life and in frequent negative press. In cities with a high murder rate, people lose their lives, families grieve, and neighborhoods are traumatized. In addition, the city as a whole suffers when people and firms alarmed by the news decide to locate elsewhere. Given that violence tends to be concentrated in minority areas, ongoing violence perpetuates stereotypes, and upper- and middle-class people limit their interactions with poor minorities even when they are members of minorities themselves. The absence of interaction and understanding contributes to mistrust and division. Those cities that fail to address their crime problem will have great trouble escaping poverty.

Many wealthy and educated workers choose to live outside the center city in commuter suburbs where the quality of life is higher. These suburbs often feature newer and larger homes, lower tax rates, better schools, and lower crime rates. While these workers typically have to trade off more time spent commuting for a higher quality of life, they can take advantage of the good jobs and entertainment amenities that center cities offer while avoiding the challenges of living in those cities. In spring 2020, many educated workers engaged in remote work to minimize their risk of getting COVID-19. Going forward, many firms are now considering allowing their workers to continue working remotely full-time or two to three days a week. This effectively reduces suburban commute times and further encourages center city workers to live in the suburbs if the center city's bundle of amenities is unappealing.

When skilled workers suburbanize, this raises the likelihood that their employers will relocate from the center city to the suburbs. Office space is cheaper in the suburbs, and a reduction in commute times from a suburban home to a suburban workplace means that these employers will be better able to retain such workers and hire them at a lower salary. As this dynamic plays out, the center city loses significant tax revenue, which lowers the quality of center city public services.

Urban Governance

Local government plays a central role in determining the trajectory of a city, as described in chapter six. The investments that local governments make in schools, neighborhood services, and infrastructure help determine the local quality of life. City governments raise revenue primarily through property taxes, especially in cities with high poverty rates where income taxes generate relatively little revenue. As a result, if the local housing market is depressed, the city has less access to funds.

Chapter six explores the urban governance challenge. None of the cities we study has had a Republican mayor in the last 30 years. In our cities with de facto one-party rule, the Democratic Party has determined the ballot of mayoral candidates and other elected government officials. Mayors often have particular powers in determining patterns of economic development and land use. They also often have direct tools they can use to reduce crime and improve public schools.

Mayors seeking reelection think strategically about how to proceed. If voter turnout is low in neighborhoods with high poverty rates, mayors have less of an incentive to address the challenges those neighborhoods face. In this way, low electoral turnout can result in a mayoral mandate that answers to relatively few constituents. It also enables corruption.

At the same time, short political terms can make mayors reluctant to test new ideas and be honest when their policies fail. Interest groups with a stake in the status quo can stand in the way of experimentation. Do the mayors of these cities have the right incentives to enact policies that attract good companies and skilled workers and improve the quality of life of the poor?

Promising Trends

An urban renaissance is playing out across the United States. Both young adults and baby boomers want to live, work, and play downtown. In recent years, several major cities, ranging from New York City to Chicago to Washington, DC, have enjoyed significant comebacks. Chapter seven presents an overview of positive trends now playing out in other cities around the country and asks whether our six cities could undergo similar revivals.

Environmental progress has sharply reduced air, water, and land pollution. Our six cities feature significant natural beauty as they are located close to bodies of water. In recent years, the Inner Harbor in Baltimore has been built up, and much past industrial blight has been remediated. Pittsburgh has been revitalized as a consumer city along the Allegheny Riverfront. Such walkable green neighborhoods attract a new generation of urbanites to live, work, and play in such areas.

The era of big data has increased local government accountability. In recent years, many cities are creating open-data web portals to share more data about emerging hot spots of crime in the city and to trace the geography of service provision ranging from garbage pickup to reports from 311 (a system through which citizens can report neighborhood problems) about local quality-of-life issues such as broken traffic lights. This diffusion of real-time data about quality of life both informs locational decision-making and provides the information that citizens need to hold their elected officials accountable for service delivery. This helps to build trust in government because officials have an increased incentive to deliver quality service.

The Fork in the Road

Our six cities seem to be stuck in a cycle of poverty, as people, businesses, and governments underinvest. There is a cruel irony here since each of these key actors can justify their choices to underinvest. However, these individually rational decisions represent a collective failure to help their respective city achieve its full potential. Our cities are poorer, and their residents have a lower quality of life and are less upwardly mobile, than what could be achieved through new investment in skill acquisition, business formation, neighborhood improvement, and quality-of-life upgrade. Violent crime and poverty are both a cause and an effect in the cities we study. The current equilibrium ensures the persistence of poverty and racial inequality. The final chapter in this book asks how this equilibrium can be broken.

Each of these cities faces many challenges around urban poverty. We believe that major reductions in the rate of violent crime could unleash the vitality of these cities. At a time when city living is in high demand, these cities are poised for a comeback. But companies and people are fearful of violent crime in these cities and have alternatives in other cities and nearby suburbs.

Real estate developers face new investment opportunities in our six cities, but they must make a bet. They could purchase cheap land and develop it now to sell at a profit later. However, they face considerable place-based risk owing to uncertainty over the local economy, crime, pollution, local leaders, and the tax rate. The rational strategy when faced with such uncertainty is to delay investment. Unfortunately, if all developers choose this strategy, the city is less likely to boom.

The six cities we focus on in this book would do well to learn what works from peer cities. They can experiment with programs and policies that have proven successful elsewhere and fit them to their local context. By building on success and being honest and open about past policy failures, our cities can begin to determine the local recipe for growing the economy and improving quality of life.

Rising city tax revenue would create the possibility of a grand bargain. Social scientists have identified a number of interventions in the lives of the urban poor that are likely to be cost effective. Providing childcare for disadvantaged children with the goal of supporting language, motor, and cognitive development, as well as encouraging prosocial behavior and providing basic medical checkups, helps such children achieve their full potential.[1] Some mayors have been able to enact these programs. For example, legislation mandating prekindergarten education for all children in New York City was a significant and popular investment in human development and well-being. Mayor Bill de Blasio was able to enact this costly legislation because of New York City's economic vitality. As a new generation of young people acquire better skills, a solid middle class can emerge.

An urban economics approach emphasizes binding budget constraints. In summer 2020, our local, state, and federal governments faced increasing budget deficits from the ongoing COVID-19 pandemic. Even if state and federal officials transfer large amounts of money to struggling cities, these officials will face significant limits on their ability to offer such funds in the medium term. This cruel logic suggests that it is unrealistic to believe that the federal government or major private foundations will fund the investments required to revitalize these cities.

At a time when these shrinking cities are spending a large amount of money to honor past pension obligations to retired city workers, they have a limited capacity to invest in cost-effective policies like early childhood education. This logic suggests that there is an imperative for these cities to improve their economic performance.

Our six cities compete with other cities to attract and retain people and jobs. In recent history, these cities have been losing this national competition. The history of these cities influences the mindset of current residents, yet it also defines the urban landscape. An aging housing stock and transportation infrastructure was built decades ago and has since been underinvested in.

While history matters, expectations also play a key role in determining investment by the public and private sectors. Throughout this book, we introduce ideas from urban economics that are familiar to academic economists but not to the general public. One of these ideas is *coordination failure*: this happens when independent but interconnected decision makers underinvest and move too slowly to reverse historical trends. Few are willing to be a first mover in investing in future success. However, the future of these six cities is not written in stone. If the private and public sectors were to make more investments in people and neighborhoods, then residents and firms would follow suit, guided by the belief that there is a bright future ahead.

The historical obstacles that our six cities must overcome to enjoy economic success are immense but not insurmountable. The right set of investments in people and places will unlock the full potential of these post-industrial cities. This book presents a pathway for identifying and implementing such strategies and also provides a set of quantitative benchmarks for judging whether these cities are truly experiencing a comeback.

NOTE

1. García, Heckman, Leaf, and Prados 2017.

2

Long-Run Trends in Poverty

Our six cities differ from the average US city. They are older and have lost population and jobs over the last several decades. They have a lower percentage of whites relative to the national average and a higher share of their populations living in poverty. This loss of population and increase in poverty have had a variety of effects on the demographic indicators we present in this book.

The six cities are at different stages of their economic development. While each has suffered from population loss in recent decades, and while each still struggles with poverty, Philadelphia and Pittsburgh have undergone economic comebacks that distinguish them from the other four cities. Later chapters will look at the economic, political, and sociological factors that help explain the divergences among these cities and between our six cities and the nation as a whole.

Population Decline and Poverty

Many people are "voting with their feet" and choosing not to live in one of our six cities. Over the past 50 years, the US population grew by 52 percent, but these cities shrank by a total of 38 percent (figure 2.1). Measured in percentages, Detroit experienced the largest population decline and Philadelphia experienced the smallest. (Figure 2.1 and other demographic figures in this chapter draw on US Census Bureau data from 2010 because data from the 2020 census were not available at the time of writing. We believe, however, that the demographic trends we have identified are unlikely to have changed dramatically in the past decade.)

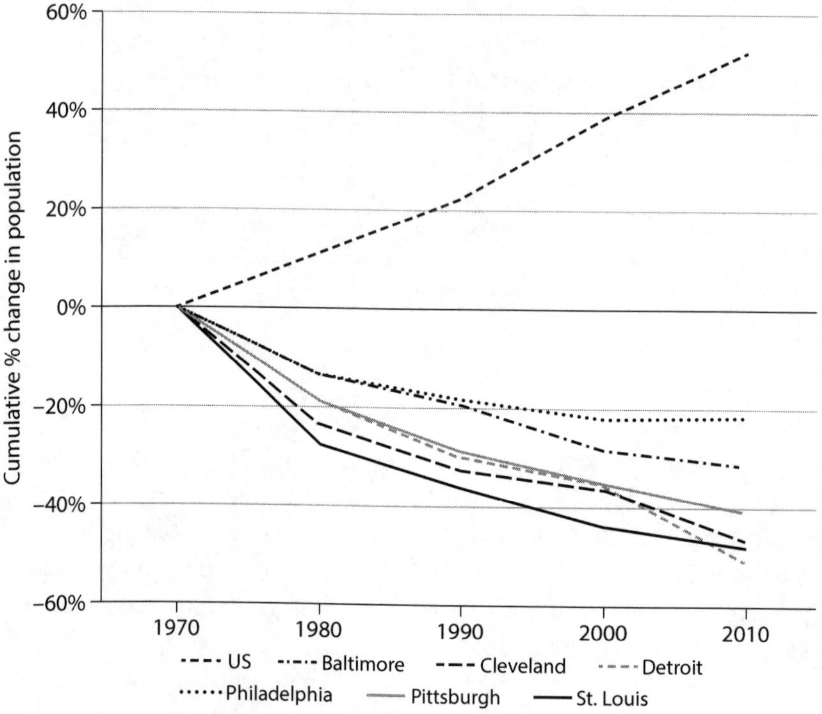

Figure 2.1. Compared with the nation as a whole, each of the six cities has lost population over the past half century.

Researchers have tracked population change and poverty across counties over time to document the correlates of local change.[1] Geographic areas with colder winters and lower levels of college graduates in 1950 grew more slowly from that year to 2000. The cities we study fit this description, with cold winters and less-educated adults.

The poverty rate for all our cities increased from 1970 to 2010, with the greatest percentage increase occurring in Detroit (figure 2.2). While the national poverty rate increased from 1970 to 2010, the increases were much larger in our cities.

A city's poverty share can increase over time because non-poor people leave, poor people move there, or the new generations born to poor families remain poor. The same is true for areas within a city. For example, between 1990 and 2010, 45 percent of census tracts in Detroit witnessed a five or more percentage point increase in the share of their population living in poverty

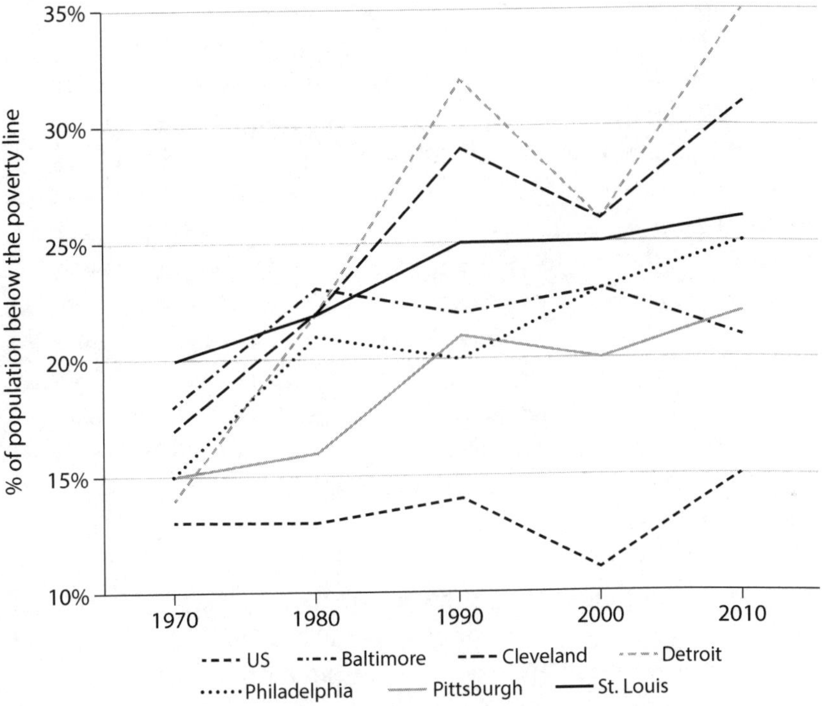

Figure 2.2. The poverty rate in each of the six cities has grown more than has the US poverty rate.

compared with 34 percent of census tracts in Baltimore. At the same time, nearly half that number of census tracts in Detroit witnessed a five percentage point or more *decrease* in the share of their population living in poverty, whereas 25 percent of census tracts witnessed this same decrease in Baltimore. This means that substantially more neighborhoods in Detroit witnessed increases in poverty than decreases, and the same was true in Baltimore, although to a lesser degree.

The poverty data actually understate the poverty challenge because many young African American men are in prison. One study estimated that 20 percent of Baltimore City's young Black men were in jail in 2005.[2] If these young men were not in prison, they would likely add to the overall poverty rate in Baltimore.[3]

Another way to measure how the six cities have fared is to compare how they have changed relative to their immediate suburbs. From 1970 to 2018,

Detroit became much poorer compared to its immediate suburbs. Over this period, the share of residents living below the poverty line in the city grew from a 10 percentage point difference with its suburbs to a 22 percentage point difference. In 2018, 36 percent of people in the City of Detroit lived below the poverty line while 14 percent of people living in the city's immediate suburbs lived below the poverty line. In 2018, all six of the cities had a more than 12 percentage point difference with their respective suburbs in the share of residents living in poverty.

While poor households are increasingly segregated in US metropolitan areas, so too are the wealthy. In his book *The New Urban Crisis*, Richard Florida finds that the wealthy are more segregated than any demographic group investigated. Calling this increasingly persistent crisis the "Big Sort," Florida demonstrates that different types of segregation (e.g., income, education, and occupation) reinforce one another.[4]

All our cities have lost population as people moved to other places in the United States. But all have gained immigrants from outside the United States. However, only in Allegheny County, Pennsylvania, where Pittsburgh is the county seat, was there positive net migration from 2010 to 2018. Wayne County, where Detroit is the county seat, experienced the greatest losses. Unfortunately, the US Census Bureau provides data only about the education level of migrants moving into cities, not about migrants moving out. Although educated people have been moving to our cities, we do not know how many of them stayed over time.

The population identifying as African American in each decade from 1970 to 2010 was much higher in our six cities than the US average. The percentage of Blacks in these cities also increased more than it did for the nation as a whole. For example, African Americans made up 12 percent of the US population in 1970, rising to 14 percent by 2010. Over the same period, African Americans grew from 43 percent of the population in Detroit to 84 percent, 38 percent to 55 percent in Cleveland, and 20 percent to 28 percent in Pittsburgh.

Each city's percentage of college graduates has risen in the past half century, as was the case for the nation as a whole (figure 2.3). But the cities also show clear disparities, with Philadelphia, Baltimore, and St. Louis near the national average of college graduates and Pittsburgh exceeding the national average, while Cleveland and Detroit have less than half the national share. Four of the six cities made substantial progress from 2000 to 2010, while the other two made less progress.

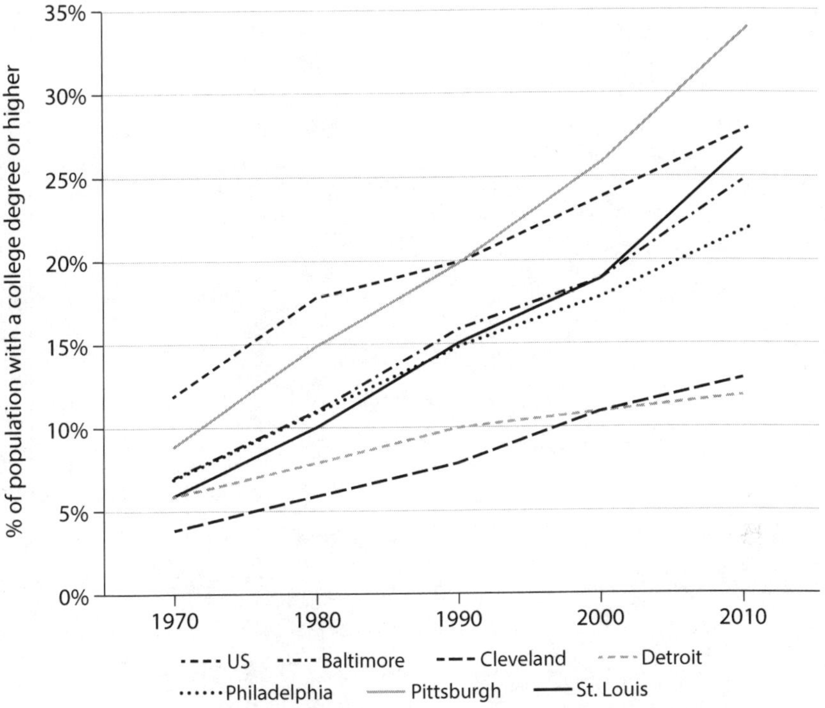

Figure 2.3. The percentage of the population with a college degree or higher has risen in the past half century but has risen more in some of the cities than in others.

However, these data do not tell the whole story. We are actually seeing a "tale of two cities." St. Louis, for example, has both a high poverty rate and a high percentage of college graduates. While 34 percent of people over age 25 had a bachelor's degree or higher in St. Louis in 2017, 37 percent had a high school degree or less. This means that the city has both a significant population that is highly educated and relatively affluent and a large population that lacks a college degree and lives in poverty.

The Geography of Concentrated Poverty within the Cities

Data at the level of census tracts can be used to measure the geography of poverty in cities. In all six of our cities, the census tracts that are farther from the city center generally have lower poverty rates (figure 2.4).[5] Neighborhoods that are close to the city center tend to feature older housing

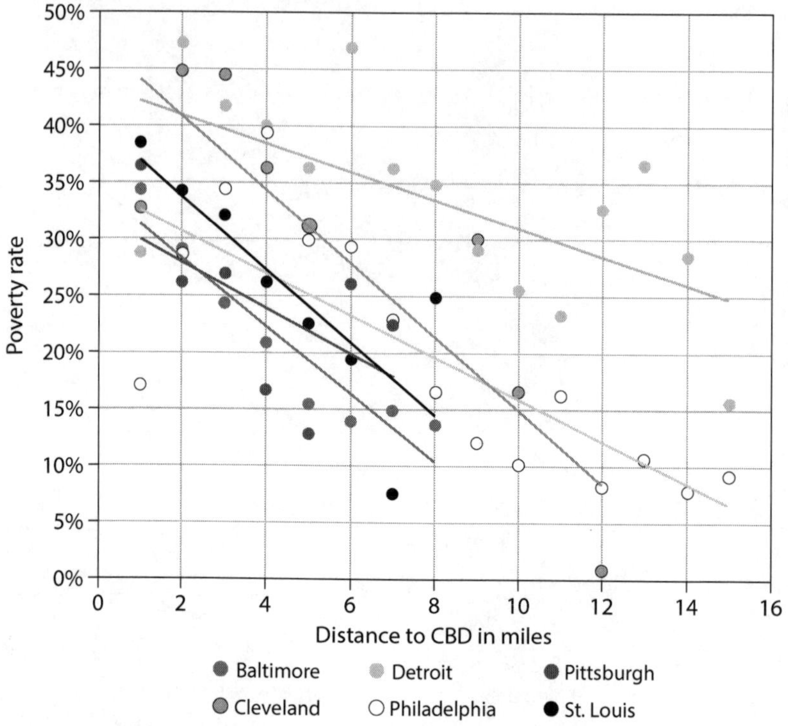

Figure 2.4. Census tracts that are farther from the central business district (CBD) tend to have lower poverty rates than those that are closer. Census tracts are grouped by one-mile increments from the CBD using 2010 data.

stock because that is where the city was originally built. At the same time, proximity to the city center is desirable in vibrant cities because that tends to be the location of many jobs and shopping opportunities.

Philadelphia has the lowest poverty rate close to the city center—just above 15 percent—while the other cities range from about 30 percent to 40 percent. This suggests that Philadelphia's city center has witnessed more revitalization than those of the other cities. Across all six cities, poverty declines with distance from the city center, with scattered exceptions. Detroit features the flattest gradient of poverty relative to distance, and Cleveland has the steepest gradient.

Poor people can only afford cheap housing, which is usually older housing stock of lower quality where landlords have not invested in upgrades. Unfortunately, there is growing evidence that living in such older housing may increase the likelihood of remaining poor because of exposure to toxins like lead. Chapter five returns to this link between poverty and living in older housing.

The traditional version of the American Dream is that the United States is a land of opportunity where the child of a poor adult can become rich later in life. Census tract data cannot be used to study intergenerational income dynamics for specific families. Fortunately, a project at Harvard's Opportunity Insights lab is studying this issue. A research team led by Raj Chetty has access to the Internal Revenue Service's tax database, which has allowed them to link the income data of parents to the income of their children. By knowing the parents' home address and the ages of their children, the team can determine where the children grew up. The team compared the household income rank for children born between 1978 and 1983 with the mean earnings of those same individuals in 2014–15, when the children were young adults. They then ranked neighborhoods on a scale of 0 to 1, with neighborhoods closer to 1 having higher average incomes.

Our six cities do not score well on this upward mobility index. The median county-level ranking for economic mobility in the United States is 0.419. Only one of our cities, Pittsburgh, is near this level, at just above the median of the county distribution. Cleveland is at the 17th percentile of the country distribution, while Baltimore is at the 2nd percentile. This means that 98 percent of all counties in the United States have higher economic mobility rates than Baltimore City.

Declining Center City Investment

While the number of housing units constructed in the previous decade has trended upward for the United States, it has generally gone down for our six cities (figure 2.5). The number of new houses being built in the United States in the previous decade nearly doubled from 1970 to 2010 while the number being built in our cities declined between 44 percent and 78 percent. The largest decline was in Detroit, and the smallest decline was in Baltimore. Low rates of new housing construction indicate that investors do not view the area as offering strong growth potential. This means that the housing supply will age over time, just as a population with low fertility rates will age over time.

Even if few new homes are being built, urban economists have argued that existing homes will be renovated as time passes because older housing

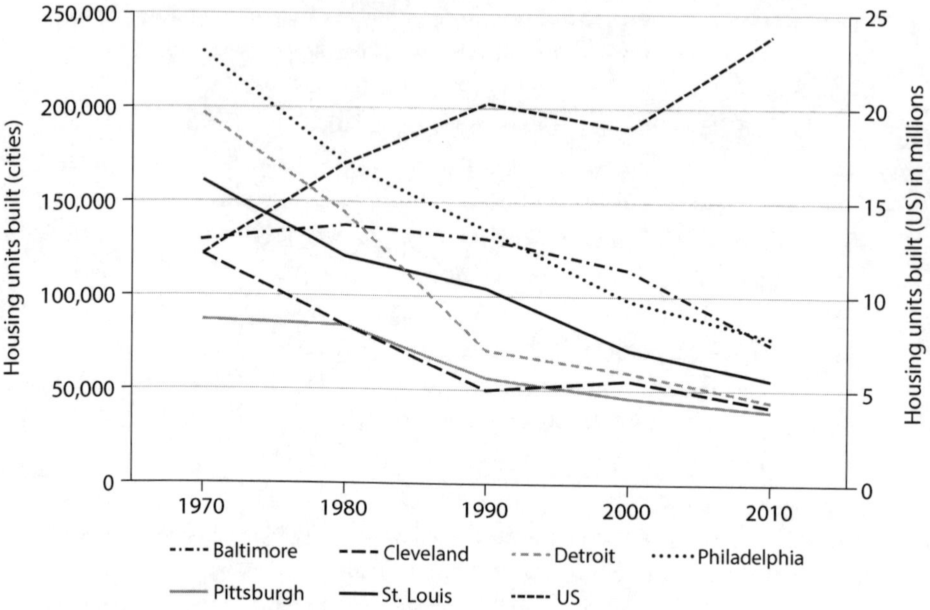

Figure 2.5. The primary vertical axis (*at left*) represents the number of housing units built in previous decades in our six cities. The secondary axis (*at right*) represents the number of housing units, in millions of units, built in previous decades in the United States. The number of housing units built has generally declined in all six cities, while the number for the United States as a whole has risen.

is often located close to the desirable center city. Consider old brownstone buildings in Manhattan, for example. Many rich people buy these and renovate them. This has also happened in downtown Philadelphia. The period covering 2000 to 2010 witnessed the gentrification of many downtown neighborhoods in the United States, with increases in the number of college-educated whites and poorer minority households leaving for the suburbs to pursue better labor market opportunities and different amenities than downtowns offered.[6] Our six cities experienced similar trends, as their downtowns remain some of the only areas that have seen significant private-sector investment in recent decades. For the most part in our cities, however, housing has continued to age and depreciate.

A key variable here is expectations. If potential investors expect that local neighborhoods have a bleak future, they will be less likely to purchase properties and renovate them. A type of self-fulfilling prophecy emerges as areas that are not expected to thrive receive relatively little investment.

Why Rebuild These Cities?

Given that populations in the six cities are declining, a strict libertarian response would be, "Since people are deciding to move away, why rebuild these cities?" This same issue arose in Germany in 1991. After German reunification, policy makers debated whether the best way to help East Germans was to rebuild East Germany's cities or, instead, let them continue to decline and encourage their residents to move to West Germany.[7]

At a time when the US population's migration rate is declining and the social costs of high poverty are better understood, a hard libertarian line does not have a strong case. Some people are "footloose"—the term we use to describe people and firms that are relatively free to move elsewhere—but many are stuck in place. Recognizing this point, more scholars are promoting place-based policies for stimulating local growth because they see that poor people are not able to move away from these places and that they and their children are likely to remain poor.[8]

Why are poor people not leaving our six cities? Do they love the place where they live? Do they rely on local social and family networks? Do they lack information about what life is like in places where they have never lived?

A field experiment could provide insights. Suppose the researcher offers a poor person in St. Louis a one-time payment of $15,000 to move to a more prosperous city, such as Seattle. If this person turns down this offer, then they reveal a desire for remaining in this city. If this poor person then rejects an even more generous offer of $50,000 to leave St. Louis then we can infer that they have a very strong desire to keep their social ties and connections. Such information would be useful to policy makers as well as interesting to economists. It would reveal the financial incentive necessary to encourage poor people to move to opportunity. It also would justify investing in place-based policies to help poor places grow richer if the local population has a great desire to remain living in those places.

The need to improve the well-being of poor children is an especially strong argument. Our six cities had roughly 914,000 children in 2010. The majority of these children (58 percent) live in neighborhoods with poverty rates exceeding 25 percent, and 10 percent of all children live in neighborhoods with poverty rates above 50 percent. In all six cities the proportion of children living below the poverty line is higher than the proportion of adults living below the poverty line—by at least 8 percentage points in all cities and as high as 16 percentage points in Detroit. In fact, more than half of all children in Detroit and Cleveland live below the poverty line. The poor children in these cities have much to gain if the cities can be revitalized.

Furthermore, the fate of these areas is not set in stone. The same streets that were the site of the 1968 riots in Washington, DC, now feature one-bedroom apartments that rent for $2,500 a month.[9] What are today poor areas of our six cities often were thriving neighborhoods in the past that served a productive urban economy. They can serve that purpose again by emphasizing their natural and competitive urban advantages and by building on their existing strengths in key industries.

NOTES

1. Glaeser, Ponzetto, and Tobio 2014.
2. Davis 2005.
3. Neal and Rick 2016.
4. Florida 2017.
5. Holian and Kahn 2015; Rosenthal and Ross 2015.
6. Baum-Snow and Hartley 2020.
7. Uhlig 2006, 2008.
8. Glaeser and Gyourko 2005; Austin, Glaeser, and Summers 2018.
9. Badger and Bui 2020.

3

Urban Labor Market Demand

For most people, jobs largely determine their income. As such, the local labor market is crucial to residents' well-being. A city's labor market opportunities can grow if incumbent firms hire more workers, if new firms start up, or if the city attracts firms from elsewhere. Any firm considering locating in one of our six cities will estimate what its annual profit will be in that city relative to what its profit would be if it were located in another city, such as Portland or Atlanta. Urban economics teaches us that a firm's profit varies across cities because the price of land and the price of quality-adjusted labor varies across cities, as do the cost to transport goods to consumers and state and local taxes. Firms that use heavy inputs will seek to be closer to input providers to reduce transportation costs. Firms that produce heavy output will seek to be closer to final consumers to reduce shipping costs. Land-intensive enterprises will consider locating in areas with low rents. Firms that gain from being in proximity to other firms (due to either learning from other firms or from lower transportation costs) will seek to cluster together.[1] Firms that gain from being close to other firms in the same industry will "follow the herd."[2]

The six cities we study compete for jobs and people with every other city and suburb. At a time when hundreds of thousands of people live in poverty in these cities and are not moving to a booming city, what can be the engine of local private-sector growth? For example, the proximity of Baltimore to major eastern consumer hubs creates profit opportunities for firms such as Amazon to locate distribution centers in areas around Baltimore. Could Baltimore undergo a revival because such firms choose to locate not just distribution centers but headquarters there as well?

Recent Trends in Urban Job Growth

Local labor demand is determined by the set of firms that choose to continue to produce in a given city and what each of them produces. Local labor demand is also a function of the growth of new and incumbent firms. Firms do not make their locational choices in isolation. Competitors seek to enter markets where they face less competition.

Over the period from 2001 to 2019, only two of our six cities experienced growth in total employment: Philadelphia and Pittsburgh (figure 3.1). As explained at other points in the book, these two cities have fared better on several indicators than the other four cities.

All six cities have lost tens of thousands of jobs in manufacturing since the 1960s, ranging from a 75 percent reduction in Cleveland to a 92 percent reduction in Philadelphia, compared with a 35 percent decline in the United States (figure 3.2).[3] Manufacturing jobs now account for a tiny percentage of overall employment in these cities. Philadelphia, for example, had over 260,000 jobs in manufacturing in 1969, accounting for over a quarter of all jobs. By 2018, it had just over 21,000, accounting for just over 2 percent of all jobs.

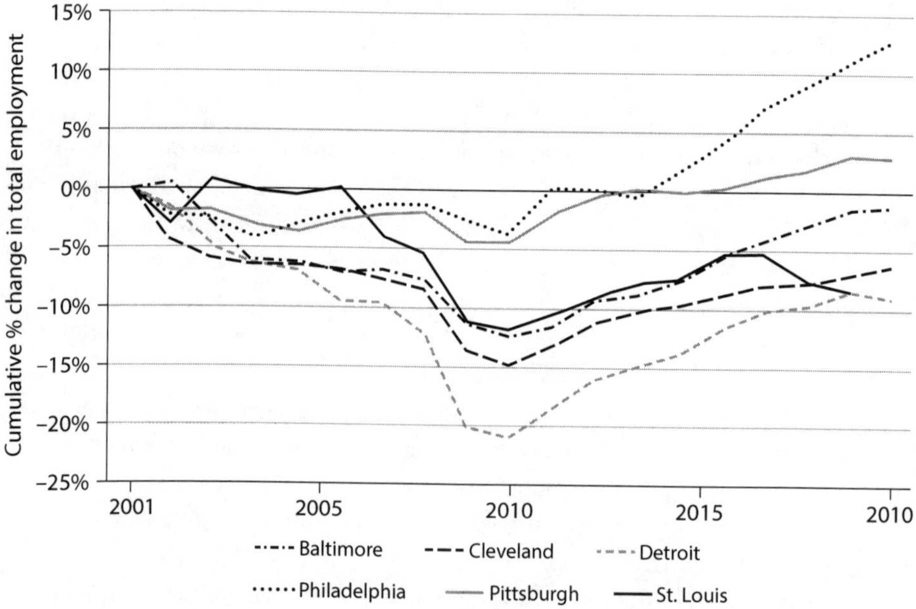

Figure 3.1. Only two of the six cities gained jobs in the first two decades of the 21st century. Source: Quarterly Workforce Indicators

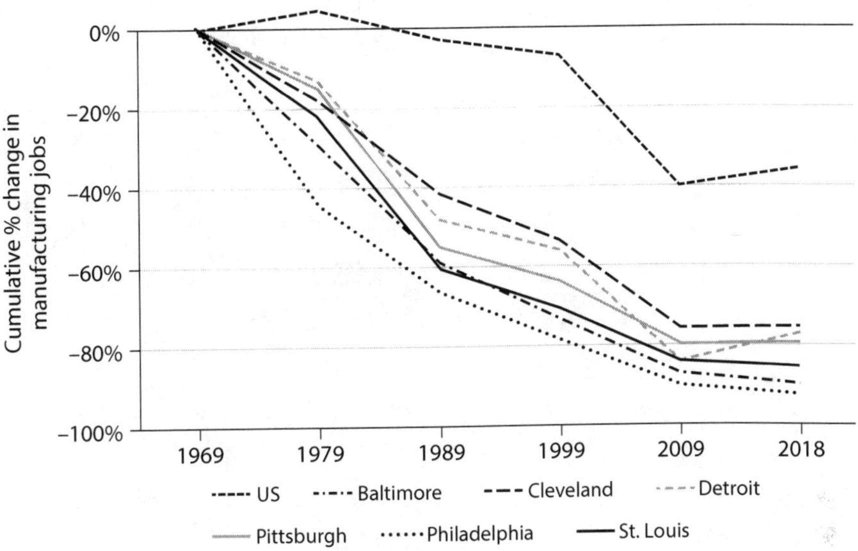

Figure 3.2. All six cities have lost most of their manufacturing jobs since 1969. Source: US Department of Commerce, Bureau of Economic Analysis

Each local economy features a different bundle of local industries. New York City has many people employed in finance, while Detroit had many people employed in manufacturing cars. Intuitively, when a city specializes in an industry that is booming at the national level, that city does well.

All the cities experienced gains in employment in health care and social assistance industries (figure 3.3). This is no surprise in cities like Baltimore, with Johns Hopkins Hospital, or in Cleveland, with the Cleveland Clinic. As dense population centers, cities have distinct advantages in offering health care services—even more so if they are nationally or internationally renowned. Biotechnology and pharmaceutical start-ups are also doing well in several of our cities, including Cleveland, Philadelphia, and Baltimore. The University of Pennsylvania in Philadelphia and Johns Hopkins University in Baltimore are leading the way, as are other educational institutions involved in pharmaceutical and medical research that has spillover effects on local industries.

Pittsburgh is an outlier among the cities with regard to these spillover effects. Research centers at Carnegie Mellon University, the University of Pittsburgh, and other institutions have spurred innovative discoveries that

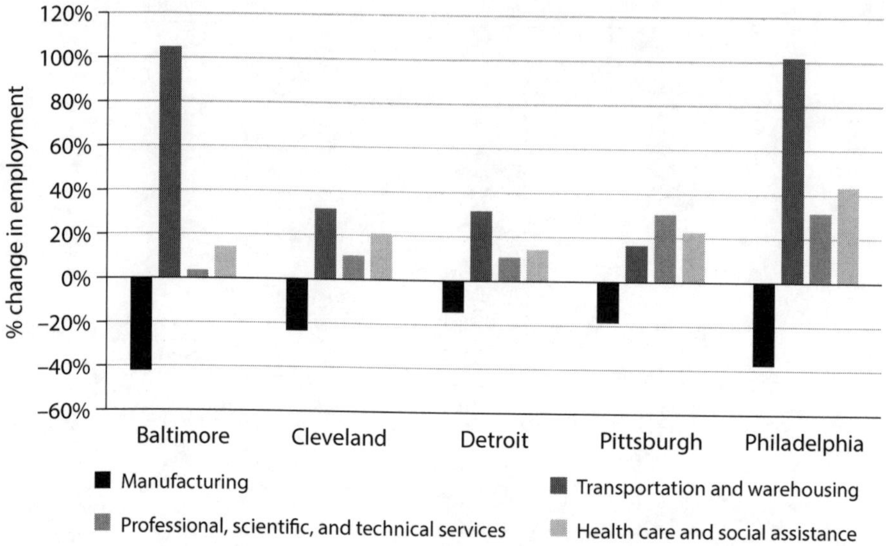

Figure 3.3. The counties containing five of the six cities (no data are available for St. Louis) saw employment in manufacturing drop from 2003 to 2018 while employment in other sectors increased. Source: US Department of Commerce, Bureau of Economic Analysis

have attracted the likes of Google, Uber, Duolingo, PNC Bank, Bayer, and others. According to a recent report from Brookings Institution, Pittsburgh has enjoyed significant growth in advanced industries involved in manufacturing, technology, and health services.[4]

The Formation of Industry Clusters and the Consequences of Success

Once a successful economic cluster forms, such as New York City's Wall Street in finance or Hollywood's entertainment cluster in Los Angeles, this tends to create a "domino effect" as new firms in related industries move there. Today, the tech boom is concentrated in five cities: Boston, Seattle, San Francisco, the area known as Silicon Valley south of San Francisco, and San Diego.[5] Such clusters are self-reinforcing. Once a cluster takes root in a place like San Francisco, other firms move there to learn from incumbent firms and draw on a skilled labor force.

When firms in the same industry are located near one another, workers can move to the area and be confident that they will face less risk of unemployment. If they lose a job at one firm, they can move to another firm in the same area. When workers face less unemployment risk, firms can pay a lower wage premium and still attract them. In this sense, labor pooling provides another reason for firms in the same industry to cluster together.

As an industry-specific boom takes place, demand for nearby real estate increases. Real estate developers in cities like Boston, Portland, San Francisco, and Seattle face severe zoning restrictions from local governments.[6] Their inability to build new housing translates into much higher home prices, which deflects people to the suburban fringe. This growth in urban sprawl exacerbates traffic congestion and reduces the local quality of life as lower- and middle-class people endure long and crowded commutes. These limits to growth in wealthy coastal cities create opportunities for rival cities, including the six cities we study.[7]

Higher cost of living means that companies need to pay workers more to live and work in expensive coastal cities. Our six cities could stand to gain as companies move some jobs to areas with cheaper housing and commercial real estate. As information technology continues to improve, firms can fragment and move many office operations away from their primary headquarters. The jobs that move away from superstar downtowns tend to be administrative jobs with standardized tasks so that one's productivity is affected less by one's immediate surroundings. In contrast, a firm might want to keep key dealmakers or its creative employees working in a city with similar workers. In such cases, the productivity of these workers increases as a function of the attributes of those who work for other nearby firms. JPMorgan Chase used to have a major foothold on Wall Street in New York City, but the company recently moved tens of thousands of jobs to lower-cost cities like Plano (Texas), Columbus (Ohio), and Wilmington (Delaware) and is considering whether it still needs to be headquartered in New York City.[8] New York City's loss could be one of our cities' gain. Indeed's chief economist Jed Kolko looked at all job postings in metro areas with at least one million people in 2017 and compared the top 10 most expensive metro areas with the remainder. His team found that construction, call center, and logistics jobs were underrepresented in pricier metro areas, although those areas still had a high share of high-skill tech and high-end service jobs.[9]

The Future of Middle-Skill Jobs

The decline of manufacturing jobs in our cities resulted in the loss of thousands of occupations that paid well for people with less education than a bachelor's degree. Along with the loss of these jobs, the real wages of less educated workers have fallen in the United States from the 1980s to the present, further exacerbating income inequality.

Young workers benefit from knowing what skills are in demand in different industries in local labor markets. No one firm is large enough for it to have a private incentive to broadly advertise what skills it is looking for in order to help workers decide whether they want to acquire these skills and then apply to work there. Many cities have quasi-public economic development agencies that can play this role of information intermediary by surveying local employers to discover what skills they need. Such information aggregation would play a useful role in helping these cities identify the "mismatch" between what skills firms are looking for and what skills residents currently have. These organizations can also provide quantitative analysis of employment trends in various sectors. The Economy League of Greater Philadelphia collaborated with the City of Philadelphia in 2017 and 2018 to publish an industry analysis to inform the city's workforce development strategy. The analysis identified several key low-skill, high-salary occupations with career development pathways, such as general office clerks and customer service representatives.[10]

The research of David Autor has shown that the nature of work in recent decades has changed more for workers who are less educated than those who are more educated. This has implications for organizations focused on training the next generation of workers, as we explain in the next chapter. The trend toward increasing numbers of high-education, high-wage jobs and low-education, low-wage jobs with a decreasing share of middle-skill occupations has been particularly strong in urban labor markets.[11] This job polarization trend has pushed low-skill workers from middle-wage jobs that have become increasingly specialized and that increasingly require differentiated skills. Instead, low-skill workers have been increasingly concentrated in low-wage jobs. In contrast, as machines now provide the muscle and computers quickly perform calculations, workers with so-called noncognitive skills, such as being a "people person" and an extrovert, receive a wage premium.

Recessions, like the one caused by the COVID-19 pandemic, accelerate job polarization and the automation of routine work. Cities and industries that suffer more from a recession are more likely to increase automation and increase the number of high-skill jobs that complement this type of automation.[12] Over the last three recessions that occurred in the past 30 years, job losses have been associated with a rise in automation.[13] This means that firms in an industry are choosing times of decline (i.e., recessions) to substitute capital such as robots or software-automated processes for less-skilled workers.

Urban economists are split on the spillover effects of living in a city with a large share of college graduates. An early finding in this literature was that every worker's wages (both high-skill and low-skill workers) are raised when the local labor market features more college graduates. In recent research, David Autor has found that the beneficial effect of living in an area high in human capital accrues mainly to the highly educated.[14] This means that high school graduates do not earn a wage premium if they live in a high-skilled city. Given that rents are higher in these cities, Autor's finding suggests that this provides an incentive for less-skilled workers to seek out cheaper cities that feature lower levels of educational attainment. In such cities, they will earn roughly the same wages and have lower rents, leaving more for other forms of consumption.

Richard Florida is well known for his work on the role of the "creative class" in sparking the back-to-the-cities movement. As Florida states, "About nine in 10 Americans with a college degree are members of the creative class, which is made up of knowledge workers in education, healthcare, law, arts, tech, science, and business. But, only six in 10 members of the creative class hold a college degree." His recent work highlighted the geography of the creative class across US metro areas and found that Baltimore, Cleveland, Pittsburgh, and St. Louis were all among the top 10 metro areas experiencing the fastest growth in creative class shares of total occupations from 2005 to 2017.[15] He partly attributes this growth to the cost advantages of affordable housing and modest improvements in the economies of these cities.

Natural Advantage

Each of the six cities was once a thriving manufacturing center that prospered because of its physical location. Their natural advantages of proximity to water and to consumer markets, accessible through their transportation infrastructure of rail, highways, and airports, still give them a cost advantage in shipping inputs in production and in shipping final output to market.

Baltimore's and Philadelphia's locations give them easy access to nearby major cities, and being near the Atlantic Ocean offers them the advantage of being port cities. Port cities have opportunities for employment and business growth in transportation and warehousing related to cargo imports and exports. Ports also provide businesses with an advantage in being able to export their goods and import supplies more cheaply. In 2017, the ports of Baltimore (7,244,013 metric tons) and Philadelphia (3,877,620 metric tons) ranked 11th and 16th in total trade for US ports.[16] This puts Baltimore close to the activity level at ports like Seattle and Miami, and Philadelphia close to New Orleans and Mobile. Philadelphia increased its total port trade by 290 percent from 2000 to 2017, while Baltimore increased its by 160 percent. Baltimore is one of only four eastern US ports with a 50-foot (15.2-meter) shipping channel and a 50-foot container berth that accommodates some of the largest container ships in the world. In addition, the expansion of the Panama Canal in 2016 made it possible for Baltimore to receive the larger cargo carriers, often from Asia, that previously were limited to the Pacific Coast. Both Baltimore and Philadelphia could consider focusing on growing industries that stand to benefit from being near large ports.

In addition to ocean access, Baltimore's and Philadelphia's proximity to Washington, DC, and New York City creates opportunities that a more geographically isolated city would not have. This takes the form of both contracting opportunities with the federal government and labor market opportunities for workers living in Baltimore and commuting to DC once or twice a week on the train. For its part, Detroit, with its proximity to Toronto, sits at the nexus of US-Canada trade. It is located near four of the five Great Lakes and is part of the US transcontinental railroad system that connects with Great Lakes port traffic. It is crossed by three major US interstate highways: I-75, I-94, and I-96. All these factors provide Detroit with an opportunity to take advantage of its ready access to markets in Canada.

The Competitive Advantage of Older Inner Cities

In 1996, Michael Porter published an optimistic piece arguing that poor center cities such as the ones we study in this book have greater economic potential than has been commonly recognized.[17] His piece focused on how to unleash the business potential of center cities. Despite the challenges in poverty and education that our six cities face, they remain excellent sources of employment for businesses that could use a workforce trained for technical careers in local community colleges.

Porter pointed to the potential of specific industries including food processing and distribution, printing and publishing, light manufacturing, recycling and reuse, business-to-business services, and entertainment and tourism. These businesses could thrive because, to be successful, they must be close to many other businesses, transit infrastructure, and high population centers. Time is more valuable than ever, and the speed at which these businesses deliver goods and services is central to their success. So their location is key to their success.

Despite lower household incomes than suburban neighborhoods, inner-city neighborhoods offer unmet local demand because of their denser populations. Suburban neighborhoods tend to be well served with strip malls and convenience stores, leaving a potential market in the inner city. Porter estimated that while the median household income in inner-city Baltimore is 39 percent lower than the rest of the metropolitan area, the aggregate spending power is nearly the same, and the spending per establishment is two-thirds greater. In addition, each of our cities has a large enough population to create demand for a range of non-tradable services that can only be supplied locally, such as doctor's offices, restaurants, car repair shops, and lawyer's offices.

Another unrecognized potential in our six cities is that of entrepreneurship. Poverty necessitates a culture of entrepreneurship in which people find creative ways to supplement their incomes in the form of microenterprises and providing social services. This often exists outside the frame of the formal economy and remains underutilized. For example, while Uber and Lyft have been growing in recent years, Baltimore has a long history of "hacking," where drivers give carless residents rides in exchange for small sums of cash. These hack drivers responded to local demand that was unmet by the taxi industry. Our cities also have a large number of social and religious organizations and nonprofits where the potential for creating for-profit industries exists. How can our cities and these organizations turn informal entrepreneurs into formal, for-profit, legal entities?

Firms Avoiding Locating in the City Center

Footloose firms pose a challenge for cities with higher operating costs in the form of taxes and regulations. These firms can move to the suburbs or to another city. In recent years, for example, Baltimore has lost several corporate headquarters, including that of the WillScot Corporation, which merged with Mobile Mini in 2020 and moved to Phoenix.

In our recent research, we have used pinpoint locations of business establishments to study their propensity to locate just outside a city's boundary. For example, if firms are located just outside Baltimore's boundary, this is evidence that firms are seeking access to Baltimore's markets but want to avoid the political consequences, in terms of taxes and services, of being in the city. Though this measure varies over time, it provides a ranking of which cities are most friendly to business. It is also a way of disentangling which policies have attracted firms to locate within city borders. For example, if a new mayor wins an election and enacts pro-business policies, this measure can be used to test whether the negative effect of being in a city declines, indicating that firms are now finding the city to be a more business-friendly place. This approach offers an alternative to other rankings such as WalletHub that rank the best and worst states in which to start a business.[18] For example, we find that Baltimore City actually reached its nadir in 1999. In the 2000s, the city's population loss began to level off, poverty rates declined, the homicide rate declined, and the number of college graduates in the city increased. Similarly, Detroit reached its nadir in 2009 after undergoing bankruptcy and suffering from some of the worst localized effects of the Great Recession.

The demand among firms for locations in center cities is changing. In an age of advanced information technology, firms don't need all their workers to be located in the same physical environment if they can collaborate online. This lowers their demand for expensive downtown commercial real estate, which lowers their costs and raises profits.

Barriers to Small-Business Growth

Much of Seattle's economic success over the last 30 years is due to the growth of Amazon and Microsoft, which were small firms just a few decades ago. For small businesses to be an engine of local growth, they must overcome many obstacles. New firms must acquire permits to operate, find a location, hire workers, sell output, and compete. Since these firms are unlikely to be selling on the national or global market, the city and suburbs must have sufficient demand for their output. As such firms grow, they must be able to identify employees with the skills to fit into the organization. To grow, firms need access to finance. Since they are unlikely to have collateral and will be seeking small loans, national banks are likely to view them as too risky and too small to be worth a bet.

High regulatory burdens can hinder firm growth. This regulatory maze is often left at the feet of businesses: they have an obligation to solve the maze rather than the city having an obligation to guide them through the process. Cities could focus more on removing regulatory barriers and less on operating incentives, since businesses stand to gain more from the former than from the latter. State and local governments need to engage in a comprehensive cost-benefit analysis of regulations and eliminate barriers to job creation and firm growth.[19] The role that navigating regulatory barriers plays in limiting firm growth could be tested by randomly assigning a regulatory "concierge" to help small businesses avoid regulatory hurdles. The program could be evaluated by testing whether the average firm that receives help is more likely to succeed than firms in the control group that do not.

Following increased legislation resulting from the 2008 financial crisis, banks have become more risk averse and are required to keep more capital in reserve to protect against economic downturns, which has led to a national contraction of lending. This hurts smaller communities more as bank consolidation has accelerated and community banks have disappeared.

In this age of machine learning and artificial intelligence, many large banks rely on algorithms to determine whether a loan is a good investment. Such an approach implicitly assumes that there is little value in soft information that is difficult to quantify but can be known from repeat interactions and an intuitive sense of the local economic environment. In such settings, local knowledge and close business relationships can foster profitable partnerships. For example, being a loyal member of a church and having an excellent relationship with the minister could be enough for a local bank official to risk making a loan, but an algorithm would not be able to quantify such intangibles. This type of lending is rare in our modern economy but occasionally is done by nonprofit lenders like community development financial institutions (CDFIs). Crowdfunding on websites like Kickstarter and GoFundMe offers another avenue for businesses to obtain start-up revenue but can only be successful for entrepreneurs with large and wealthy social networks or excellent marketing and social media skills. Business microloan sites such as Kiva, which originally began as an effort to lend to entrepreneurs in countries outside the United States, has expanded with specific initiatives in cities like Baltimore offering no-interest, no-fee loans underwritten by Kiva with loans financed by everyday people.

These small-business financing issues are crucial for creating an entrepreneurial ecosystem of shared prosperity. If more small businesses succeed, they can create an organic strategy for reducing poverty as they hire local workers.

Black-Owned Businesses and Capital Markets

Realizing the full potential of Black-owned businesses could be key to revitalizing the six cities. If cities invest more resources in Black-owned businesses and more of these businesses thrive, this success will have a positive spillover effect in African American communities. Black-owned businesses are more likely to hire Black employees, an issue we discuss in the following chapter. When there are more employers in a city, young people can engage in a job search to find the right job for them as they seek out mentors and employers they can gain from working for and with.[20] If more entrepreneurs succeed, a shift in perceptions could create a multiplier effect as more young people see that they too can become successful business owners.

Many African Americans have started businesses in our six cities, ranging from the Saint Louis Hop Shop, a Black-owned craft beer shop in St. Louis started in 2014, to Woodward Throwbacks, a Black-owned business founded in 2013 that turns reclaimed materials from abandoned houses in Detroit into a variety of household decor items.

All our cities except for Pittsburgh have a higher share of Black-owned businesses than the national average, with Baltimore City having one of the highest rates of Black-owned businesses of any US city. However, while these businesses make up a significant portion of the total number of businesses, they do not have comparable shares of revenue or employees (figure 3.4). Black-owned businesses in all our cities have around 3 percent to 4 percent of the expected share of total revenue that they would have if their share of total revenue were the same as their share of businesses. This is slightly below the national average of 5 percent. Similarly, the number of employees at Black-owned firms is 5 percent to 8 percent of the expected number if their share of employees were the same as their share of total firms. This means that Black-owned businesses in our cities, and in the nation as a

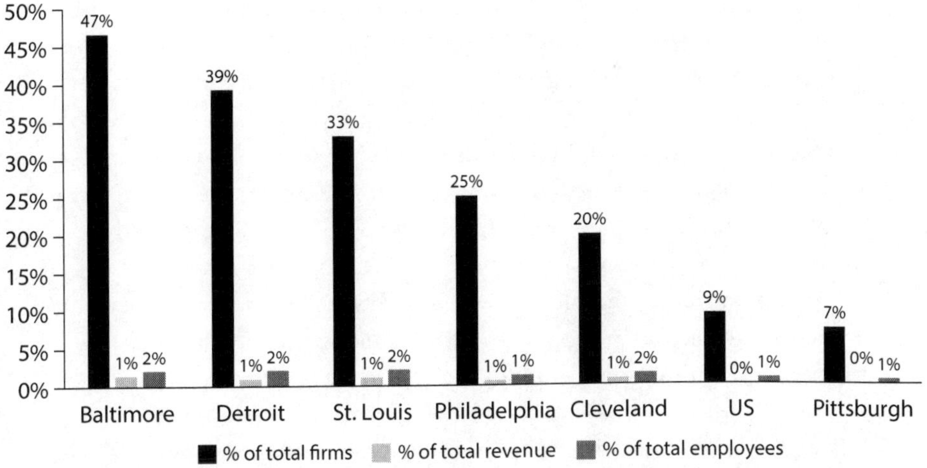

Figure 3.4. The number of Black-owned businesses in the six cities far exceeds their shares of revenue and total employees. Source: Survey of Business Owners, 2012

whole, bring in far less revenue and employ far fewer people than do white-owned businesses. In Baltimore, the total number of Black- and white-owned firms is relatively the same. Yet white-owned businesses employ 13 times the number of employees and bring in 18 times the dollar amount of revenue. The majority of Black-owned businesses in Baltimore are sole proprietorships, with 97 percent having no employees compared with 74 percent of white-owned businesses.

From 2002 to 2012, the number of Black-owned businesses in all our cities and in the United States as a whole grew by a factor of two or more, exceeding the rate of white-owned business growth. However, in our six cities, revenue grew more slowly, and the total number of employees at Black-owned firms grew much slower and even declined in Baltimore, Detroit, and Philadelphia. A recent survey by the Detroit Coalition for Economic Inclusion, a trade association for Black businesses, found that 80 percent of Detroit's top 100 Black business owners felt left out of the economic boom of the 2010s.[21] The survey also found that nearly 70 percent of these leading business owners had a negative outlook on Black business growth in 2019.

A special challenge for minority small-business owners is accessing capital. With a median net worth of $6,200, eleven times lower than whites,

Black families are less likely to have savings or housing equity owing to historical and modern-day practices of racial discrimination in home mortgage lending.[22] If minorities in these cities do not have much housing equity and therefore have trouble getting a loan, Black-owned businesses will have trouble growing. Research in the United Kingdom found that a £1 increase in the value of homes owned by a firm's directors related to a £0.03 increase in the firm's investment and that the homes owned by directors could be as important as corporate property for collateral in investment.[23]

A different approach is needed where traditional methods of measuring and assessing risk can be bypassed. A CDFI named Baltimore Business Lending began in 2017 as an offshoot of the established Baltimore Community Lending to focus on small-business lending to minority entrepreneurs. Realizing the issue of borrowers' lacking collateral, the lender provides loans to entrepreneurs with good credit but no collateral. Instead, the lender relies on a thorough review of the entrepreneur's business plan and tailored technical assistance to ensure that the loan is not risky. Similar initiatives could focus on scoring the personality traits of successful business owners to identify those entrepreneurs that have "what it takes" but lack collateral. If a city were to lead such an initiative, lenders could use their existing data to identify low-risk entrepreneurs and provide them with much-needed capital.

A family business can serve as a significant asset that can be passed on to the next generation and create wealth. Alicia Robb and Robert Fairlie have studied this issue and found that a lack of prior experience working in a family-owned business was negatively associated with business success, possibly due to the educational experience this would have provided, and that Black business owners had less of this experience than did their white counterparts.[24] They also found that Black-owned businesses have more difficulty accessing capital in start-up and early growth stages because of large differences in credit scores, with Black-owned businesses having a third of the available start-up capital that white-owned businesses do. Even controlling for credit score, Black-owned businesses are less likely to obtain the capital they need, suggesting a significant racial bias among lenders. They also find substantial differences in loan applicants' fear of rejection, with Black business owners being three times more likely to fear rejection than their white counterparts.[25]

While these figures are grim, there are stories of hope. Fearless Solutions is a Black-owned software firm in Baltimore that develops products for nonprofits and public agencies. Supported by a small-business incubator at the University of Maryland beginning in 2009, the company moved to Baltimore in 2015 and grew quickly, reaching nearly 100 employees in 2019. The business owner ascribes the company's success in part to guidance received from mentors and peer firms.[26] Could a service providing businesses with guidance from experienced mentors help other businesses in our cities grow?

Recent research highlights the challenges faced by minority-owned businesses located in majority-Black neighborhoods, which tend to experience less revenue growth than businesses in other neighborhoods.[27] If cities targeted their investments in infrastructure and other neighborhood quality-of-life improvements in areas featuring high-quality businesses in Black neighborhoods, their revenues might increase, creating a synergistic relationship in which cities could reinvest higher tax revenue in improved services.[28]

Unlocking Small-Business Potential: The Data Gap

In the above sections, we have highlighted several important issues that limit the growth of small and minority-owned businesses in the six cities we study. The local entrepreneurial environment greatly affects the success of entrepreneurs and vice versa.[29] Data gaps prevent us from knowing exactly what is holding back these businesses.

Surveys of small-business owners are essential for identifying the major hurdles they face. While local business surveys yield valuable information, they are costly to administer and can raise issues of selection bias when a nonrandom subset of people respond. In surveying a subset of a city's current business owners, it is important to note whom the survey leaves out. There may be people who are thinking about starting their own businesses, those who operate in the informal business environment, or those who are part-time business owners with full-time jobs. In addition, there are existing business owners who are thinking about expanding and opening a business in one of the six cities we study.

We do not know all of the regulations and red tape that different businesses face when starting up or growing in these six cities. We do not know the limitations of commercial real estate in different cities. We do not know the perceptions of companies located in other cities, which may be willing to relocate to one of our six cities. We do not know the extent to which banks may still be practicing implicit redlining in deploying capital in certain neighborhoods. These data gaps limit the ability of economists to target cost-effective incentives to increase private-sector job creation in our cities. By pointing out these data gaps, we seek to highlight new opportunities for a new generation of data scientists to devise new metrics for entry barriers. Such information will help local elected officials determine whether their cities can and should reform their rules to better promote local job growth.

High-Tech Start-Ups

Residents of Seattle in 1970 would be shocked to see how their city has changed with the rise of Amazon and Microsoft. Today, a new generation of start-up firms are hard at work in each of our six cities. Could one be the next Amazon?

This is an important question because all six of our cities tried and failed to attract Amazon HQ2. The offers ranged from $9.7 billion in Pittsburgh to an offer of an existing $660 million tax-increment-financing incentive to locate at Port Covington in Baltimore. Economists tend to frown on such competitions because of what is known as the winner's curse. The highest bidder in an auction for something whose value is unknown, like the economic return of Amazon HQ2, will likely overpay.

The alternative to potentially overbidding for a superstar firm is to create an economic environment that grows the next generation of star firms. The likelihood that a new firm will thrive depends on many factors, including the quality of the workforce it can recruit, the wages it must pay to attract and retain such people, and the access it has to mentors, new ideas, and venture capital. High-tech start-up firms are often spin-offs of applied research done in universities. For example, robotics companies are popping up in Pittsburgh because of research done at Carnegie Mellon University. The company Innovation Works is the largest investor in seed-stage companies in Pittsburgh, putting more than $70 million into more than 300 technology start-ups. That has attracted at least $1.8 billion in follow-on capital to the region since the seed fund began.[30]

Johns Hopkins University Tech Ventures is an arm of the university that seeks to turn translational research into commercially viable businesses. This assistance takes multiple forms, from helping businesses identify and attract financing to finding them wet-lab space on short notice. Given that Hopkins is famous for its medical school, biotech and pharmaceutical start-ups have much promise in Baltimore. Ultimately, however, much of the success of companies in Baltimore depends on the local business and entrepreneurial environment. If a business reaches growth stage and cannot find or attract a skilled manager, it may have to relocate to Boston, New York, or California.

A chicken-and-egg issue arises over tech companies' geographic choice of location and access to venture capital. Few venture capital firms will set up in small cities with a low quality of life. They seek to be where "the action is" in high-amenity areas. Start-ups that need to gain support from venture capitalists have an incentive to locate near them, and the venture capitalists seek to be close to the start-ups.[31] Given that our cities have relatively few active venture capital firms but many start-ups coming from local universities, a potential missed opportunity arises. Recognizing this dynamic, Steve Case's venture capital firm Revolution established the $150-million Rise of the Rest seed fund in Detroit to invest in underserved cities with small but promising start-up companies and environments.[32] Revolution is making a bet that getting in early will yield large returns and attract other venture capital firms to follow up with more investment.

The six cities also face the challenge of whether they are too small to be home to a nascent superstar firm. An unfortunate "minor league farm team" scenario could arise. Small cities such as Syracuse are home to minor league baseball teams but not to major league baseball teams. Baltimore will gain less from start-ups if firms start near Hopkins and then move out of the city once they boom. This out-migration is more likely to occur if such firms worry about local crime, schools, quality of life, and the capacity of the labor market to provide talent.

Companies can use seed funding to start up. But as they grow, they need more and more investment. If they cannot find it locally, they may be drawn to Boston, New York, or San Francisco, where many venture capital firms are located. However, this factor can change over time. From 2007 to 2012, only 4 percent of investors in funding rounds of $10 million or more for Baltimore start-ups were themselves from Baltimore. However, this rose to 10 percent from 2013 to September 2018, and in the first nine months of 2018, Baltimore's share was 18 percent.[33] Companies that receive investment from local sources are more likely to remain local.

Whether firms will thrive in Baltimore remains an open question. From the city's perspective, the key is to attract and retain enough start-up firms so that the law of probability guarantees that a few go on to succeed. Baltimore has seen a rise in highly skilled pharmaceutical and biotech workers but not in much else. A burgeoning cybersecurity cluster is taking shape, but apart from a handful of companies, most of them have located in the suburbs. A city can signal that it intends to build a cluster either by leveraging its local university's strengths or by gaining the investment of a major investor.[34] Baltimore is attempting to do this with its Cybertown, USA cluster at Port Covington.[35]

Another way cities can signal that they want to build clusters is to hire an economic development officer who is solely focused on one industry. The Baltimore Development Corporation has done that for cybersecurity companies. This sends a signal to firms searching for desirable places to do business that the city is both prepared and has resources to help them start up and navigate the local landscape.

This economic development strategy poses a risk, though, as a city is implicitly engaging in the managed industrial policy of "picking winners." Betting on what will be the city's next big moneymaker is less risky if the selected industry has a productivity edge there (perhaps because of synergies with the faculty and students at one of the local universities). When a city makes this type of bet, it signals that it hopes to have many other firms in the same industry located there. This points to another sort of concierge service that cities can provide businesses to help their chances of succeeding. While this service could help businesses navigate regulations, it also could provide expertise in everything that businesses are concerned with, including access to financing, workers' commutes, local hiring and contracting, marketing, and more. This type of business-friendly service would provide a "one-stop shop" for businesses, similar to New York City's New Business Acceleration Team.[36]

Given rising income inequality, there is an ongoing debate about whether local less-educated people benefit when their city attracts new high-tech jobs. One study claims that each high-tech job creates five local jobs.[37] Hairdressers, bartenders, doctors, nurses, taxi drivers, construction workers, and cashiers are examples of private-sector jobs that cannot be outsourced. These jobs will likely continue to be locally sourced if a city attracts high-tech jobs.

In Philadelphia, most recent job growth has been in low-skill jobs. Recognizing this, the Economy League of Greater Philadelphia set out to identify low-skill, high-wage occupations that provide career pathways. Jobs that fall into this category include industrial truck operators, shipping and receiving clerks, and security guards.[38] Local workforce development agencies could work with local high schools and community colleges to highlight these career pathways.

The future success of any city hinges on its fostering an environment conducive to creating sufficient labor market demand. If cities are not dynamic places of creativity where local entrepreneurs can scale successful ideas and businesses can grow, they will lose people and tax revenue to other cities. If entrepreneurs of color face barriers to entry and growth, the city loses a potentially large tax base. A city's success is also determined by its ability to supply a modern workforce with the skills that businesses demand.

NOTES

1. Glaeser 2000.
2. Dumais, Ellison, and Glaeser 2002.
3. Feyrer, Sacerdote, and Stern 2007.
4. Andes, Horowitz, Helwig, and Katz 2017.
5. Porter 2019; Moretti 2012.
6. Fischel 2009.
7. Gyourko, Mayer, and Sinai 2013.
8. Kelly 2019.
9. Kolko 2018.
10. Economy League of Greater Philadelphia 2017; Taylor 2018.
11. Autor 2019.
12. Hershbein and Kahn 2018.
13. Jaimovich and Siu 2020.
14. Moretti 2004; Autor 2019.
15. Florida 2014, 2019.
16. US Department of Transportation Maritime Administration.
17. Porter 1996.
18. Milligan 2019.
19. Glaeser and Sunstein 2014.
20. Topel and Ward 1992; Neal 1999.
21. Detroit Coalition for Economic Inclusion.
22. Fairlie, Robb, and Robinson 2009.
23. Bahaj, Foulis, and Pinter 2020.
24. Robb and Fairlie 2007.
25. Fairlie, Robb, and Robinson 2016.
26. Eichensehr 2019.
27. Perry, Rothwell, and Harshbarger 2020.
28. Perry, Rothwell, and Harshbarger 2018, 2020.
29. Glaeser, Rosenthal, and Strange 2009.
30. Linder 2017.
31. Chen, Gompers, Kovner, and Lerner 2010.
32. Konrad 2019.
33. Miller, Seigel, McComas, and Scrivener 2018.
34. Porter 2020.
35. Babcock 2018.
36. Glaeser 2015.
37. Moretti 2010.
38. Taylor 2018.

4

The Labor Supply of Local Residents

Given that many adults in our six cities do not own valuable assets, their annual income hinges on how many hours they work, their hourly wage, and any government transfers they receive. In chapter two, we documented that the poverty rate in our six cities has been persistently higher than the national average. In this chapter, we explore the challenges that young people and middle-aged people face in seeking good-paying jobs.

The Labor Supply of Young People

Every teenager makes a series of interrelated decisions concerning schooling, relationships, and planning for the future. Young people must decide how much time and attention to devote to school and acquiring human capital (i.e., knowledge and skills). They must make choices about romantic relationships, sex, and perhaps parenthood. They must anticipate the long-run consequences of their actions, which has given rise to a debate in the social sciences about their ability to be patient and avoid tempting options.[1]

The payoff to young people of achieving a given level of human capital depends partly on macroeconomic conditions. For example, if young people have the bad luck to finish high school or college when a recession is taking place, that bad timing can have permanent negative effects on their labor market outcomes.[2] Young people who go unemployed during a recession lose valuable experience and may never catch up relative to what they would have achieved if they had graduated during a boom. This research is especially relevant for the young people in our six cities because their labor markets are depressed.

Given that young people have a long life horizon, a standard prediction of life-cycle economic models is that young people will move from a weak local labor market to another market featuring greater opportunity. Events such as the 19th-century California gold rush or the fracking revolution of the last decade have been used as natural experiments to document that young men move "to where the action is" as they seek out prosperity.[3] While moving away from home imposes costs, the economic model predicts that the flow of higher annual earnings in a better labor market more than compensates for this short-run sacrifice. This logic raises the question of why more African American young people who live in the depressed neighborhoods of the six cities choose to remain there. As we discuss in the next chapter, cheap rents and social networks in these places are powerful forces that anchor them to the place they know.

Interviews with Baltimore youth, conducted by Stefanie DeLuca after the April 2015 unrest that followed Freddie Gray's death, indicated that many youth in Baltimore aspired to leave the city.[4] They saw their futures elsewhere and spoke of a lack of opportunity in the city. But given low mobility rates, the reality is that few will be able to leave. Their ability to move to a better neighborhood is limited by their bank account, knowledge of neighborhoods where they could move, and reliance on social networks. When they are able to move, it is often to another neighborhood with similar characteristics.[5]

Young African Americans in our six cities face special challenges. Many have not grown up in two-parent households. Many have single parents who work multiple jobs to make ends meet and do not have the same amount of time and resources that wealthier families do to devote to their children's well-being. Their neighborhoods tend to be poor and racially segregated. Many of the places where they live and play have toxic legacies of lead and other pollutants.[6] The schools they attend are poorly funded because of the low property-tax base in their city. Many have experienced violent traumatic experiences like witnessing shootings at a young age. Together, these risk factors raise the probability that they will not perform well in school or graduate from high school. Past studies have documented that targeted early-life interventions can foster skills and the emotional self-control needed to enter the modern workforce. But these programs are costly and many inner-city children have not had access to them.[7]

Racial Discrimination in Labor Markets

Ongoing research in labor economics explores the consequences of labor market discrimination against African Americans. Some employers may engage in taste-based discrimination because they or their employees do not want to work with certain groups of people. In this case, such employers will face higher costs for hiring workers because they limit the pool of eligible applicants. Employers who do not discriminate are able to hire quality workers at a lower wage. This logic suggests that a rise in Black entrepreneurship would attenuate this social challenge because Black bosses would be less likely to engage in taste-based discrimination against Black workers. Research bears this out, as Black business owners and hiring managers are more likely to hire Black applicants than are their white counterparts. One study found that, fearing this rejection, 19 percent of white-owned firms received no applications from Black job seekers compared with only 3 percent of Black-owned firms.[8]

A second type of racial discrimination that occurs in the labor market is statistical discrimination. This arises in cases where an employer lacks full information about any one worker and imputes to an individual the attributes of the average person in that group. This leads to a type of perverse extrapolation: a potential employer of a young Black man might believe that the applicant is more likely to have a criminal history because of the employer's perception of the average young Black male. One study found that "ban the box" policies, which restrict employers' ability to ask job applicants about their criminal history during the initial stages of a job application, had the unintended consequence of leading to increased discrimination against Black males. In the absence of full information about an applicant's history, employers assumed that most Black men had criminal histories.[9] Such statistical discrimination reduces the likelihood that young Black men are offered jobs, and this in turn reduces their incentive to learn the skills at school that would make them better competitors in the labor market. Why bother studying hard in school if employers will not reward you with a good job?

To measure the extent of this racial discrimination in the labor market, researchers replied to job ads posted in Boston and Chicago newspapers with fake résumés that had Black- or white-sounding names. The résumés that had white-sounding names received 50 percent more invitations for interviews, with little evidence that employers were accounting for socioeconomic characteristics.[10] A solution to addressing this discrimination would be to increase the number of Black-owned businesses in a city. An increase in the number of Black-owned businesses could result in increased labor market demand for Black workers.

Racial discrimination in labor markets extends outside firms. Charles and Guryan found that African Americans earned less in states where survey respondents revealed greater antipathy toward Blacks. This increases negatively as the share of the workforce that is Black rises in a given state. This employer discrimination can lead to a significant lifetime earnings loss between $34,000 and $115,000, measured in 2008 dollars.[11]

The Importance of Role Models

Many inner-city youth lack local role models and mentors who are college graduates and work full-time. Such role models would help to expand their imagination about different careers and the possibility of their becoming wealthier by investing in their education. Robb and Fairlie found that a lack of experience working in a family-owned business is associated with worse business performance outcomes.[12] Exposure to inventors and innovators can have a similar effect on children. Researchers found that children in the highest-income families are tenfold more likely to become inventors as those in families below the median income, even after controlling for test scores. They also found that growing up in a family or neighborhood with a high innovation rate in a specific technology leads to a higher probability that the child will be a successful innovator in that same technology.[13] This implies that if we were simply able to expose children to more innovators and inventors, they would have a greater chance of succeeding.

William Julius Wilson has argued that an unintended consequence of African American suburbanization has been that inner cities have lost valuable role models. As higher income minorities leave center cities, young people who remain are less likely to see and interact with adult men who work and have achieved upward income mobility. Research in development economics has documented, with data from the Dominican Republic, that when young people are informed about the wage gains that are possible by obtaining more education, this information increases their educational attainment.[14] The explanation for this is that young people are more likely to underestimate the economic benefits of education when they never interact with people who look like them and have also attained a high level of education.[15] The suburbanization of upwardly mobile people thus has social consequences for peer effects in the inner city.

Upward Mobility and the American Dream

The Opportunity Insights mapping project has taught us that our six cities have many neighborhoods where there is little evidence of the American Dream for young people. Many poor children are not wealthier when they become young adults. By linking Internal Revenue Service records for the same person over time, and thus observing where the person grew up as a child, we can learn which urban neighborhoods offer little upward mobility. However, we do not learn *why* neighborhoods differ with respect to their ability to uplift young people. Given that families choose where to live within a city, there is a fundamental challenge to disentangling the role of the family versus that of the neighborhood in shaping the life course of a young person.

To answer this question requires better data that trace milestones in a person's life and so let observers examine how certain events shape young people's growth and success. Suppose that for each teenager in our six cities, we could observe where they lived each year from birth to their current age, who lived in their household with them, what schools they attended, and who their teachers and peers were. A researcher could then use machine learning to identify the correlates of early-life success. For example, key outcome variables could be graduating from high school and earning a middle-class salary as a young adult. Using longitudinal data sets with many variables, researchers could begin to calculate probabilities: For those who grow up with two parents in a low-lead and low-stress neighborhood, how much higher is their chance of graduating from high school? The challenging part of such research is explaining differential success rates. What is the relative importance of growing up with two parents versus growing up in a low-lead and low-crime area?

Some city and state agencies collect such data in partnership with universities. In Houston, for example, researchers at Rice University partnered with city officials to standardize various databases to allow them to be merged. The Houston Education Research Consortium at Rice University's Kinder Institute merged data from various education and workforce agencies to analyze the postsecondary and workforce outcomes of public school students who began eighth grade in 1998. The researchers then used these data to compare student outcomes over 17 years in Harris County, Texas.[16] They were also able to partner with Houston Independent School District to implement a randomized controlled trial with more than 10,000 students to investigate the causal effects of arts education, reductions in disciplinary infractions, and writing achievement.[17] This kind of research offers policy makers a rigorous evidence base from which to devise policies better designed to achieve the outcomes they seek. In other cities, this remains a work in progress as different city and state agencies possess different pieces of this important puzzle.

Attempts to create big urban data sets are more than an academic exercise. They open up the possibility of understanding how young people can escape urban poverty. Baltimore's "Squeegee Kids" exemplify this challenge. Interstate 83 is the major highway that commuters use to travel to the heart of Baltimore. Young men assemble at traffic lights on off-ramps, and when cars stop at a red light, they start washing their windows and asking the drivers for money in return. Tourists, suburbanites, and business owners have complained that they feel harassed by these young people. But these youth demonstrate a willingness to work and an entrepreneurial drive. The problem is that they are working in an environment that offers no path to advancement. They are not in school and are not building useful skills. Should Baltimore pay these young people to take entrepreneurship classes led by mentors, with the goal of developing their skills and channeling them into legal for-profit businesses?[18]

Sociology research yields important insights into how to provide young people with avenues to success. For example, using data from the 1997 National Longitudinal Study of Youth, researchers found that students under the age of 15 were more likely to stay in school if they were exposed to a balance of a technical career education and a core academic curriculum. Blacks and young women are more likely to get jobs through school contacts than from relatives. In the absence of school connections to jobs, young people of color have greater difficulty finding quality jobs.[19] But work experience for youths is associated with higher earnings later in life. These findings have important implications for how junior high and high schools craft their curricula.

Young men in high-poverty areas face decisions about entering the drug trade. They know that local job opportunities for them are not good. If young people do not expect to have a long life, they will take more risks.

They will be more likely to smoke, use drugs, and engage in violent criminal activity. If young men do not know working-age men who work in a legal industry, this absence of role models will affect their decisions. If young men view drug dealing as their best occupation and as a means to support their families, they will not pay attention in school and will acquire less human capital. Many face the choice of becoming involved in the drug trade or taking low-skill service jobs that provide little income to invest in their own skills or those of their future children.

The Baltimore Police Department made 19,862 arrests in 2019.[20] Almost a quarter of these were of people aged 14 (the youngest) to 24, and 82 percent of the young people arrested were African American. Given that the 15- to 24-year-old African American population in Baltimore was around 56,000 in 2017, and that over the course of 10 years the Baltimore Police Department will have arrested almost 50,000 Black youth at the present rate, a significant portion of this demographic will have an arrest record, even after accounting for multiple arrests of some of the same individuals.

Young Black men who are arrested and jailed face a slowdown of skill accumulation, reduced labor force participation, and an increased risk of not being trusted once they are released after having served jail time. At a time when firms seek new workers but also worry about liability risk, their safe strategy as employers is not to offer these young men another chance.

These statistics are concerning, but there are some positive trends. The ongoing movement to "ban the box" aims to allow these young men to start again.[21] Incarceration means that children grow up without a father, and this increases the risk that the cycle of poverty will continue.[22] Nationally, the juvenile incarceration rate fell by half in the past decade.[23] As fewer young adults are arrested, what does this mean for the success of children in our cities?[24] The bottom line is that choices made by teenagers have lifelong effects on their standard of living.

Crime and economic development are closely related. If our cities had more job opportunities for teens, fewer teens would engage in criminal activity. They would study harder in school because they could imagine a more remunerative future in the workforce. One way to quantify this optimistic hypothesis would be to randomly offer teens at risk of becoming criminals a "good job." If gainful employment reduces crime, those randomly assigned jobs should be less likely to be subsequently arrested. A more difficult scientific study would be one that engineers a local boom so that students currently in high school become more optimistic about their work prospects. If they see good private-sector jobs that they can apply for, would they invest more effort in school? Jensen and Miller were able to conduct such a study in rural India by paying call center recruiters to visit randomly selected villages, where they conducted recruiting sessions for jobs that required at least a high school degree. Parents responded by pushing their children to do better in school.[25] In this sense, local economic development, skill formation, and crime reduction all reinforce each other.

Challenges Faced by Young Women

Young women in these cities also face significant challenges in achieving their goals. Our cities have a significantly higher share of single women living with children than does the nation as a whole. Baltimore, Cleveland, and Detroit all had more than double the national share in 2018, with Baltimore at about 50 percent and Cleveland and Detroit both at almost 60 percent.

In interviews, young mothers tend to cite several primary factors related to their decision not to marry or to delay marriage. Many low-income single mothers say that they need a spouse who makes substantially above minimum wage, has job security, and wants to retain a job or find a better job. When young men have few legal employment opportunities, they become less desirable partners, and marriage rates decline.[26] Factors other than money are equally important, such as a distrust of men, fear of domestic violence, and the importance of maintaining control over household decisions. Many young women expect to have a child as a teenager. This affects their investment in their own human capital and the time they have available to work. These financial and social barriers to marriage are often enough to keep single mothers single, even if they expect to find a suitable husband at the time of a child's birth.[27]

The child support system can make the challenges of single motherhood worse. While this system works for most American families by making sure that parents support their children, some policies do more to punish fathers than to help children. In one Baltimore zip code, parents owe an estimated $33 million in child support payments.[28] This high level of debt can often result in fathers being imprisoned or losing occupational licenses, which makes them less able to support their children.

Every year, millions of Americans rely on a variety of social insurance programs, ranging from Medicaid to the Special Supplemental Nutrition

Program for Women, Infants, and Children to the Supplemental Nutritional Assistance Program to the earned income tax credit (EITC). Critics of these programs argue that they are costly and ineffective. The Aid to Families with Dependent Children (AFDC) program was in effect from 1935 to 1997, when it was replaced by the Temporary Assistance for Needy Families program. Labor economists have argued that the rules embedded in AFDC discouraged working.[29] The EITC is meant to remove this disincentive effect. Under the terms of the EITC in 2019, people out of the labor force received nothing, but workers saw their credit rise with their earnings up to a point, followed by a gradual reduction and eventual disappearance once their income exceeded $15,570 for a single head of household. The research literature provides overwhelming evidence that the EITC has a positive role in raising the labor force participation rate for single mothers.[30] Recent research has also argued that a $1,000 increase in the EITC leads to an 8.4 percentage point decrease in the share of families that are 100 percent below the federal poverty level and that the Census Bureau's Supplemental Poverty Measure may underestimate the anti-poverty impact of the EITC by almost 50 percent by not taking into account behavioral effects.[31]

Childcare and day care are expensive, largely because they are labor intensive, highly regulated (with states like Massachusetts mandating a caregivers-to-infants ratio of one to three), and have high rent when located in real estate in higher-income neighborhoods. Yet the benefits of high-quality childcare are overwhelming.[32] The Economic Policy Institute estimates that the average annual cost of infant care in Maryland is $15,335. As many young mothers in our cities are unable to afford formal day care centers, they must rely on relatives to help out. This limits their ability to search for a job and work regular hours. If young mothers are unable to work or if a majority of their income goes to childcare, this increases the chance that their children will grow up in poverty. The Study of Early Child Care and Youth Development in the 1990s found that high-quality childcare was positively correlated with improved behavioral and cognitive outcomes at a later age.[33] However, this study also found that children who spent more than 10 hours a week in paid care at a young age had more problem behaviors, which was evidence that quality childcare is key to good developmental outcomes.

Investments in the parenting skills of low-income families have shown significant positive effects in reducing childhood behavioral problems and in raising parental efficacy. Several studies on the efficacy of the Chicago

Parent Program, a 12-session training program for parents with children aged two to four, found that one year after the training, parents used less corporal punishment, reported greater self-efficacy, greater warmth, and a reduction in child behavioral problems compared with a control group.[34] Research on a similar intervention in Jamaica in the 1980s that focused on parent interaction with children to develop cognitive and socioemotional skills found that the training increased earnings of the children by 25 percent 20 years after the intervention.[35] These studies provide evidence that well-designed and funded early childhood programs can have significant benefits for both parents and children.

The Labor Supply of Middle-Aged People

In our cities, many middle-aged adults are out of the labor force. Factors contributing to this lack of participation include substance abuse, health problems, and government safety-net programs that could have the unintended consequence of discouraging work.[36] People who are out of the workforce have trouble maintaining their skill levels. A person's propensity and ability to find a job decrease the longer the person has been unemployed. An optimist would posit that such displaced workers can be retrained so they can work in a booming sector. We often hear, for example, about retraining coal miners to be computer programmers. But labor economists who have studied the performance of job training centers have been pessimistic about the possibility that a large number of unemployed workers can be cost-effectively retrained for a new career.[37] Their core argument is that, as we age, most of us have less ability to reinvent ourselves and learn new skills.

Many people who are out of the workforce are struggling with behavioral health issues that prevent them from entering the workforce, as happened with the rise in opioid addiction in the 2000s. The good news is that the national rate of opioid prescriptions peaked in 2012 and has since steadily declined, a statistic that holds true for all our cities (figure 4.1).

Although this decline sounds promising, the numbers include only retail opioid prescriptions; they do not include the illegal drug trade. Baltimore, for instance, had a consistently lower rate of opioid prescriptions than the national rate, lower than that of any of our other cities during the same period. Yet in 2017, the city witnessed 761 drug- and alcohol-related overdose deaths, 692 of which were from opioids. This was the highest overdose fatality rate of any city in the United States, and the annual

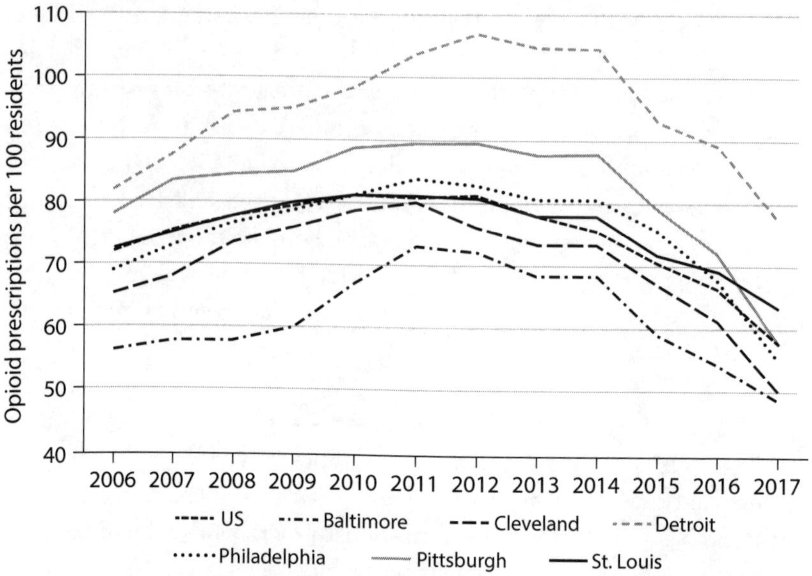

Figure 4.1. The rate of opioid prescriptions per 100 residents, by county seat, rose and then declined for the six cities and for the United States between 2006 and 2017.

number has more than doubled since 2014.[38] From 2015 to 2017, all our cities had higher opioid-related death rates than the national rate (figure 4.2), with the recent spike in opioid death rates almost wholly attributed to the rise of fentanyl, a synthetic opioid of far greater potency than pure heroin. Opioid addiction remains a serious and unsolved public health crisis that has widespread implications for the well-being of all residents.

Labor and urban economists have emphasized two reasons why middle-aged workers may have trouble finding work. Some are out of the loop and not aware of opportunities or of how to prepare for jobs.[39] A person who is unemployed and has unemployed friends is unlikely to hear about new opportunities because social networks are key to finding a job.

Others have trouble accessing job opportunities because of high transportation costs. Access to fast transit in cities, whether by car or by nearby public transit, is crucial for one's quality of life.[40] In our cities, the number of households with no vehicle available in 2018 was more than double the national rate and as high as triple the national rate in Philadelphia. Poor minorities tend to live in neighborhoods distant from employment centers

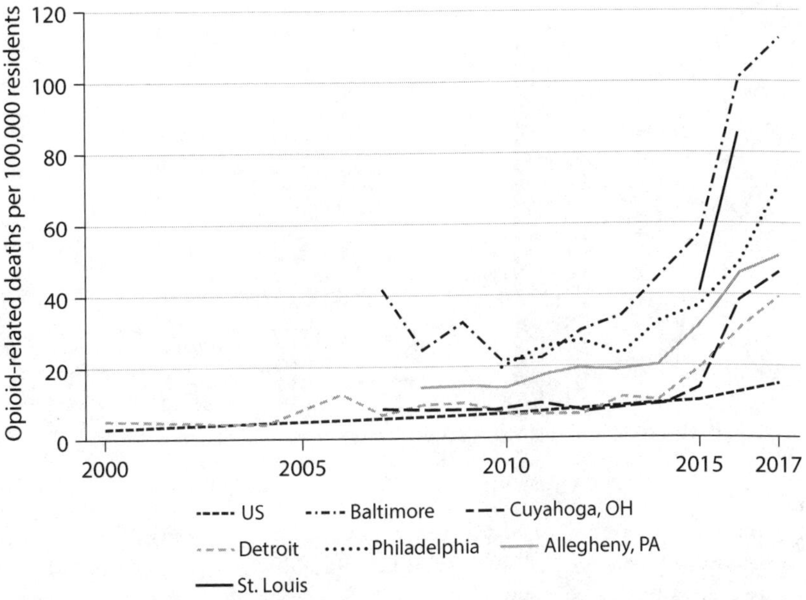

Figure 4.2. The rate of opioid-related deaths per 100,000 residents has skyrocketed since 2015. Sources: Centers for Disease Control and Prevention and state, county, and city health departments

and do not enjoy easy access to reliable public transit. The spatial mismatch hypothesis posits that limited access to transportation increases minority unemployment.[41] In effect, commuting costs act as a tax on working and leads people to work less, making them more likely to be unemployed. Slow and unreliable public transit involving multiple bus changes can further discourage people from working.

Philadelphia and Cleveland have far superior light rail infrastructure than that of our other cities, with Detroit falling far behind (figure 4.3). Philadelphia also performs better in providing transit access for African Americans relative to the overall population of the city and is the only city with a higher percentage share of African Americans within half a mile of a light rail station than the rest of the population.

There is also an information mismatch wherein people searching for jobs are often disconnected from formal and informal networks of information about the jobs available. Given that people rely on their friends and families for job information, less-educated people who live in high-poverty

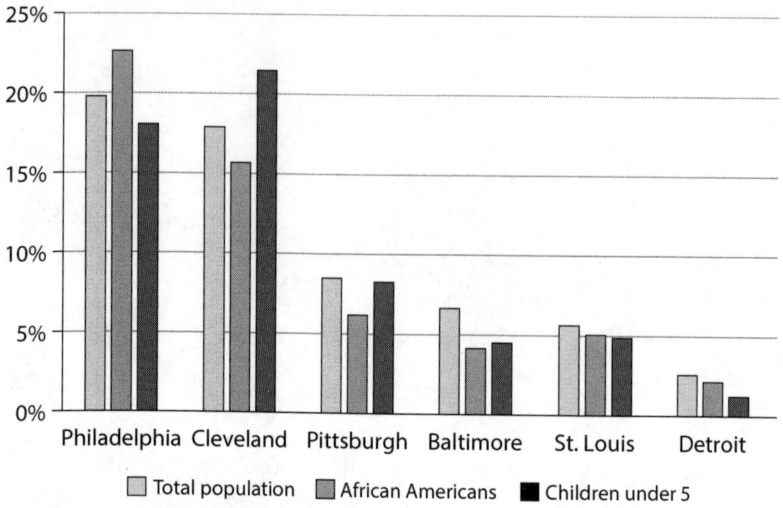

Figure 4.3. Philadelphia and Cleveland have the most extensive and accessible light rail networks of the six cities. Philadelphia's light rail is accessible to African Americans, while Cleveland's is accessible to families. Source: Authors' calculations using shapefiles of state and city light rail networks

neighborhoods are more likely to be uninformed and have more trouble searching for the right job for them.[42] In contrast, those who have attended elite schools and colleges are more likely to have friends who can help them search for good jobs.

In the modern economy, more and more people are participating in the gig economy by working part-time for Uber or other app-based businesses. In our cities, though, such jobs are less likely to be part of a middle-aged worker's work strategy, as fewer people in our cities own cars. The gig economy is a two-sided platform: having a supply of gig workers (such as in food or dry-cleaning delivery) requires that enough people living nearby demand their services. Since these cities are poor and their populations are shrinking, the overall demand for gig suppliers is low.

Skill Mismatch?

Many of the adults in these cities are not well trained, causing them to live in poverty. There is a mismatch between their skills and what the modern workforce wants.

In each of our cities, active for-profit and nonprofit sectors are seeking to raise workforce skills. Ideally, private-sector firms would communicate to suppliers of the labor market exactly what skills they need from new employees and present a pathway so that people who develop these skills will be hired. This pathway should incentivize the suppliers to focus their efforts on building the skills the firms want. Unfortunately, it now appears that many of the job-skill suppliers are not meeting the market test, given that many adults are living in poverty and not working.[43] Local community colleges could be filling this role, but many lag behind in adequately training a future workforce.

Given that community colleges are nonprofit, it is surprisingly difficult to benchmark them with respect to whether they are doing a good job of boosting young adults' skills. Put simply, we do not have a control group that could show us what a motivated 25-year-old who attends one of these schools would have achieved in skill formation had this person attended a different school instead. If these skill suppliers were private firms, on the other hand, we could check to see whether they are raising tuition prices and still attracting more students. This would be a market test for proving their services are in demand.

Given that many young people are remaining in our low-opportunity cities, there is an open question about their career ambitions. Would young people in our cities invest more time and effort in school if they foresaw meaningful careers? If they had the resources to start their own business and had role models who had already achieved this, how would their trajectories change? If obstacles to achieving this dream were minimized, would more seek out self-employment? If the answer is yes, then occupational licensing is a costly barrier to entry.[44] While incumbent firms benefit from facing less competition, legitimate questions surround the optimal permitting system for judging when a new entrepreneur is prepared and qualified to receive a license to offer services.

Debating the Merits of an Urban "Big Push" for Labor Demand

Relative to the nation as a whole, the urban labor markets in the six cities are underperforming. On the supply side, the workforce lacks human capital. Both the urban young and middle-aged face challenges that reduce their ability to participate in meaningful work. On the demand side, modern companies are not locating in these cities, and small firms face constraints on growing.

Faced with these realities, advocates of place-based interventions sometimes call for a "big push." A famous example is Jeffrey Sachs's Millennium Villages Project.[45] In poor villages in rural Africa, Sachs introduced several synergistic interventions aimed at improving the health, education, and incomes of local people. In a modern US city, however, such an intervention would be expensive, and determining which high-poverty areas would receive special treatment would generate distributional debates.

Given the poor prospects for a big push in US cities, we present a thought experiment to stimulate debate. During a time of low interest rates, our cities could borrow money to engage in an enormous public works campaign that would employ at a living wage every unemployed able-bodied resident.[46] Such a Keynesian local stimulus would increase the short-run deficit, but the resulting employment surge would bring benefits. The city's public goods would be improved as trash was hauled away and run-down areas were restored. If newly employed people actively engaged with their work, rather than viewing it as free money, their work readiness and their self-esteem would rise. Their children would see role models working and actively engaged in society. Similar programs have existed in cities like San Diego, Chicago, Denver, and Seattle, but they have been on a small scale.[47]

Such a big push would be costly. In 2017, around 24,500 people were unemployed in St. Louis. If each of them were paid a living wage of $15 an hour plus benefits, it would cost the city roughly $1 billion a year. In fiscal year 2018–19, St. Louis's budget was just over $1 billion, meaning that it would need to double its annual budget to pay for this program. While there would be savings in terms of a lower demand for social services, policing, and jailing and in improved tax revenue from increased consumption, these would have to be weighed against the significant costs.

In our discussions with Italian economists, they have warned us that this is a bad idea. They point to southern Italy and the high rates of public employment for much of the population.[48] They argue that a culture of dependency has been created and that little innovation or risk taking is occurring.

In this age of big data, the output of public-sector employees could be measured to judge whether a public employment campaign improves a city's quality of life. However, other questions would arise. Would a public-sector push increase or decrease private-sector investment in the city? A full-employment program would decrease the labor pool for the private sector, driving up the cost of doing business. If crime declines, investment might increase. Would crime significantly decline as young people foresee future careers for themselves? Would school quality and neighborhood peer effects improve with more working adults living in these communities?

Debating the merits of a big push for mass employment stretches our imagination about alternative strategies for helping our cities' residents maximize their potential. One theme of this book is that our cities have not experimented enough with different policies and with ex post rigorous evaluations of these policies to learn what works. As we have laid out in this chapter, understanding the societal determinants of what stimulates the growth of human capital is quite complex. A whole host of factors affects skill formation and labor market outcomes, including the quality of life in a person's neighborhood, which we will explore in the following chapter.

NOTES

1. Becker and Murphy 1988; Cameron and Heckman 2001.
2. Oreopoulos, Von Wachter, and Heisz 2012.
3. Clay and Jones 2008; Feyrer, Mansur, and Sacerdote 2017.
4. Poverty and Inequality Research Lab at Johns Hopkins University 2017.
5. Greenlee 2019.
6. Currie, Zivin, Mullins, and Neidell 2014; Currie, Davis, Greenstone, and Walker 2015.
7. García, Heckman, Leaf, and Prados 2016.
8. Stoll, Raphael, and Holzer 2004.
9. Agan and Starr 2018.
10. Bertrand and Mullainathan 2004.
11. Charles and Guryan 2008.
12. Robb and Fairlie 2007.
13. Bell, Chetty, Jaravel, Petkova, and Van Reenen 2017.
14. Wilson 2008, 2012; Jensen 2010.
15. Ross 2011.
16. Houston Community Data Connections 2018.
17. Bowen and Kisida 2019.
18. Rodricks 2019.
19. Plank, DeLuca, and Estacion 2008; Rosenbaum, DeLuca, Miller, and Roy 1999; Tach and Edin 2011.
20. Open Baltimore, BPD datasets.
21. Doleac and Hansen 2017; Agan and Starr 2018.
22. Addo, Sassler, and Williams 2016.
23. Horowitz and Carlock 2017.
24. Goldstein and McMullen 2018.
25. Jensen and Miller 2017.
26. Waite and Gallagher 2001; Autor, Dorn, and Hanson 2018.
27. Edin 2000. Gibson-Davis, Edin, and McLanahan 2005.
28. Wenger 2020.
29. Moffitt 2019.
30. Nichols and Rothstein 2016.
31. Hoynes and Patel 2018.

32. Gormley, Phillips, and Anderson 2018.
33. Anderson 2010.
34. Gross, Garvey, Julion, Fogg, Tucker, and Mokros 2009; Breitensten, Gross, Fogg, Ridge, Garvey, Julion, and Tucker 2012.
35. Gertler, Heckman, Pinot, Zanolini, Vermeerch, Walker, Change, and Grantham-McGregor 2014.
36. Autor and Duggan 2003.
37. Heckman 1994.
38. Baltimore City Health Department.
39. Hellerstein, Neumark, and McInerney 2008.
40. Raphael and Stoll 2001.
41. Kain 1968.
42. Ioannides and Loury 2004.
43. Dworak 2019.
44. National Conference of State Legislatures 2020.
45. Sachs 2012.
46. Alesina, Baqir, and Easterly 2000.
47. City News Service 2018.
48. Alesina, Danninger, and Rostagno 2001.

5

Urban Neighborhood Quality of Life

Each of our six cities is a mosaic of neighborhoods. A person who lives in a high-poverty neighborhood and does not work experiences a very different city than does someone who works full-time and owns a home. Given that rents and home prices are higher in the best parts of a city, richer people will tend to live there. This creates a physical separation of the rich and poor within the city, leading to neighborhoods segregated by race and income.

In this chapter, we seek to understand the quality-of-life opportunities for the rich and poor in our cities of interest. If a city offers the successful little in the way of quality of life, they will move to other cities or work in the city but commute from the suburbs. As a result, the city's stores and its tax base will suffer. People will have different qualities of life depending on where they live, work, and play within a city.

At a time of rising income inequality, understanding the challenges that poor people face in terms of neighborhood quality of life is essential. Given that poor people live in neighborhoods with the lowest quality of life, inequality is actually underestimated in this nation because it does not factor in the greater crime and pollution risks that poor people face.

Living and Working in the City versus the Suburbs

In the early 20th century, when within-city transportation was slower and more expensive, people lived closer to their jobs, and the vast majority of jobs were in the city center. With the advent of cheaper automobiles and the federal construction of freeways in the 1950s, more and more people suburbanized as middle-class and rich people sought new and larger homes.[1] The Second Great Migration that brought Black populations from the South to northern cities increased the share of Black residents in our cities, and racist fears propelled even more whites to the suburbs. As more people suburbanized, jobs started to suburbanize. These trends meant that many people lived and worked in the suburbs while a smaller number lived and worked in the city. In some high-amenities cities, people live in the city and reverse commute to the suburbs. These commuting flows matter because as the educated and wealthy have more residential options, they can avoid the center city. This raises the quality of life of the middle class and wealthy but further isolates the urban poor while lowering the average tax base of center cities.

The COVID-19 pandemic in 2020 caused many firms to allow skilled workers to work remotely. Telecommuting means that someone can live in a less expensive city like Cleveland and work in a city with more jobs like San Francisco. In 2018, while 37 percent of jobs could be done entirely at home, only 25 percent of employed people worked from home for some amount during the typical day.[2] Going forward, more people can live in cheaper cities like Philadelphia and Baltimore and telecommute to cities with better job markets like New York City and Washington, DC, enabling workers occasionally to take the train to office headquarters for important in-person meetings. Working from home also opens up the potential for greater gender equality in the workplace as more women could enter the workforce if allowed the flexibility to work from home.[3]

The Locational Choice of the Rich

Educated people tend to marry other educated people. High-income couples may seek luxury housing with easy access to the amenities of cities. Relatively short commutes to a local labor market featuring a diverse mix of industries and occupations mean that neither spouse must sacrifice career ambitions.[4] These realities limit the ability of medium-sized cities to compete in attracting more of these couples. Our six cities do not offer the same scale of employment opportunities as major local labor markets such as New York City, San Francisco, or Los Angeles. High crime rates in our cities further reduce their competitiveness in attracting and retaining such high-income couples.

When the upper middle class and wealthy suburbanize, they do not intend to exacerbate the center city's poverty. Rich people have little incentive to take into account that the average income of the city declines slightly when they move to the nearby suburbs. In his classic 1970 book *Exit, Voice, and Loyalty,* Albert O. Hirschman contends that those who leave a city (exit) can protect themselves from weak governance rather than engaging in "voice."[5] The two strategies are interconnected. If an upper-class household believes that it has little influence (voice) with a mayor in influencing schooling and policing policies in the city, an alternative strategy for accessing local government services that meet the family's desires is to suburbanize. If the wealthy can avoid taxation by moving outside the center city, sending their children to private schools, or having their own private security, they have less of a stake in city institutions such as policing and public school quality. This disengagement from center city civic life contributes to the persistence of weak local institutions. For example, if parents are not sending their children to public schools, they have less of an incentive to support school infrastructure upgrades and may vote against politicians and ballot measures to that effect.

Each of our six cities has stately mansions. These durable homes are old and were built at a time when people had larger families. Relatively few dual-earner households desire a five-bedroom 19th-century house when an alternative is a new, smaller apartment located downtown. In recent years, educated women have been marrying later and having fewer children. This means that large homes built for the successful 1950s family are not a good match for the modern couple who may have a single child. These individuals want to live, work, and play downtown, where high-quality apartments and the best entertainment and dining options coexist.

While some rich people do live in cities, they are often isolated from poor neighborhoods through choices they make to limit their physical interactions with strangers. Their children attend private schools. They use private transportation. They socialize at private clubs and expensive restaurants. Such individuals minimize their time spent in public places. Implicit in these choices is a lack of trust in strangers.

Parents might consider sending their child to an urban public school, but they may worry that a single disruptive child in the class would detract from their child's education. If rich parents believe that peer effects influence their child's development and that poor kids are on average worse peers than rich kids, they will engage in a type of statistical discrimination and try to have their children in classrooms without poor children.[6]

A Tale of Two Cities

Each of our cities is home to both poor and rich people. The growth in income inequality has accompanied a growth in income segregation by neighborhood.[7] Housing rents are low on average in our cities, and they are extremely low in some zip codes in our cities (figure 5.1). Only two zip codes in our cities have median house values above $500,000, and 49 zip codes have values below $100,000, 27 of which have values below $50,000. By way of contrast, in December 2019 the median value of a home in California was over $500,000.

Our six cities are old. Cleveland, for example, was founded in the year 1796. Given that Cleveland's population is shrinking, the durable housing stock ages each year, and there is relatively little new investment in the poorest part of town to upgrade the housing stock. Redlining effectively prevented major housing investments in Black neighborhoods in the 20th century, as the federal government steered banks away from lending in communities where the majority of residents were Blacks or immigrants. As a result, large areas of our cities have lacked significant upgrades to the housing stock in recent decades. As the older capital stock depreciates, cheap rents act as a poverty magnet. Poor people living in old deteriorating housing contribute to a city's reputation for "grime," which creates a marketing challenge for a city competing for talent with other cities.

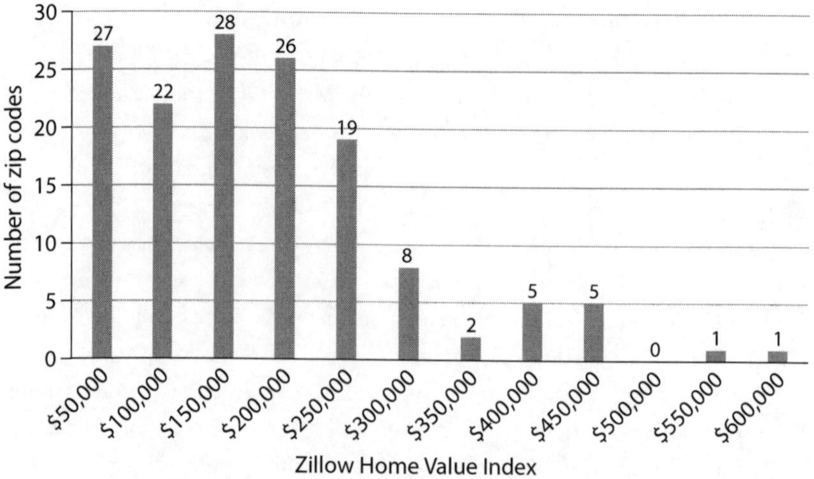

Figure 5.1. The Zillow Home Value Index by zip codes show that the six cities have plenty of cheap housing and relatively little expensive housing. Source: Zillow, https://www.zillow.com/home-values/

Wealthy and poor neighborhoods can be physically close together but look and feel worlds apart. Take the case of two Baltimore neighborhoods, Harlem Park and Roland Park. Roland Park features large mansions with lawns, few commercial spaces, and quiet tree-lined roads. Harlem Park features vacant rowhouses, abandoned lots, trash-strewn streets, and payday loan stores and was near ground zero for Baltimore's 2015 unrest. The two neighborhoods have a nearly 20-year gap in life expectancy but are less than five miles apart.[8]

Causes of Neighborhood Racial and Income Segregation

In 1970, 734 census tracts in our six cities had populations that were 0 to 20 percent African American, compared with 326 tracts in 2010 (figure 5.2). In 1970, 290 tracts had populations that were 80 to 100 percent African American compared with 579 tracts in 2010. Clearly, the count of heavily concentrated African American neighborhoods has grown over time. An optimist can also see that the count of integrated neighborhoods has grown slightly.[9]

The causes of residential segregation emerge from a dynamic process that accelerated over the course of the mid-20th century. The Second Great Migration of the 1940s to the 1970s, which witnessed the migration of millions of Black families from the South to the North, prompted a reaction

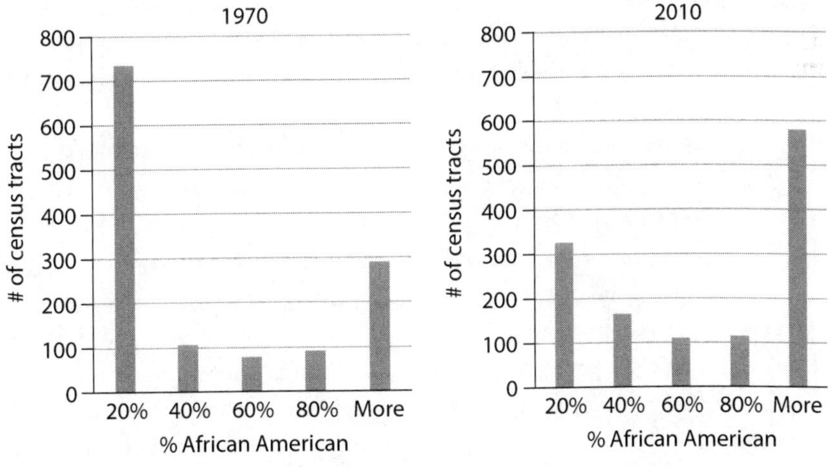

Figure 5.2. The African American share of the population in census tracts in the six cities grew between 1970 (*left*) and 2010 (*right*).

among white families that extended beyond neighborhood segregation.[10] Increases in the number of Black families in northern cities also corresponded with an increase in the number of white families enrolling their students in private schools and moving to the suburbs, and increases in spending on policing, higher crime and incarceration rates, and greater neighborhood segregation, beginning as early as the 1960s. This dynamic meant that Black families did not enjoy large gains in neighborhood quality of life after their migration.[11] An open question is whether middle-class and richer families would react similarly if poor minority families moved into their neighborhoods on such a scale in modern times. Proposals to expand Section 8 housing vouchers and programs such as Moving to Opportunity are gaining momentum and, if widely adopted, could result in a similar outcome with millions of poor families moving into wealthier neighborhoods.

Federal and local housing policy of the early to mid-20th century effectively prevented African Americans from living in neighborhoods with whites, creating racially segregated neighborhoods. White flight and racist real estate practices in the 1960s and 1970s further enforced the racial divide through practices like blockbusting, where residential real estate agents, stoking the racial fears of white homeowners, convinced the owners to sell their homes at a reduced price and then resold those homes to incoming Black families at increased prices.[12] The persistence of racial segregation in modern times is exacerbated by the fact that African Americans have lower incomes than whites and a fraction of the wealth. Blacks continue to face discrimination in the contemporary mortgage finance market and in the real estate market.[13]

In addition to the Federal Highway Act of 1956 facilitating suburbanization through the construction of $25 billion worth of freeways, which often were built over and through Black communities, the federal government built millions of units of public housing from the 1930s to the 1980s near the center of cities. Suburban and white political enclaves protested proposals for construction of new public housing units in their neighborhoods, resulting in the federal government locating them in mostly poor minority neighborhoods.[14] Given that the residents of public housing units are mostly poor, the siting of public housing served to isolate the poor in cities and in certain neighborhoods within those cities, further concentrating poverty in urban American.

The net effect of all these factors is that Blacks are more likely to rent and to choose from a smaller menu of residential options than whites with similar incomes.[15] Once many Black families have moved to a neighborhood, a type of path dependence begins. A Black neighborhood forms, and the "easy" path is for more Black families to continue moving there. Recent research in urban economics has found that once such a community has taken root, institutions such as churches and stores that cater to this group open there, which reinforces those living there to remain.[16]

The 2008 recession had a large impact on Black homeownership rates in the United States, which fell to levels similar to those before the passage of the Fair Housing Act in 1968. As of 2016, the Black homeownership rate was 41 percent, compared with 71 percent for whites. This lack of progress has significant implications for intergenerational transfer of wealth, which is an important source of future investments in education and housing.[17]

Another cause of residential segregation is where public housing is sited within a city. In Philadelphia, around 80,000 people live in public housing, most of whom are poor. This means that around 20 percent of Philadelphia's poor people live in public housing.[18] Economists have studied how poor children's quality of life is affected when they grow up in neighborhoods of concentrated poverty. The findings suggest that children do worse when they grow up in concentrated poverty such as that found in public housing.[19] A child who grows up among other poor children is less likely to be exposed to role models who work and pursue advanced education. On average, the peer effects in such high-poverty areas are likely to be worse. Negative peer effects reduce the likelihood that such children will graduate from high school and go on to enjoy early career success.

Using data from Boston, Cleveland, Detroit, and Philadelphia, researchers found that the existence of public housing units was related to significant increases in neighborhood poverty in the following decades.[20] Recent research by Eric Chyn has shown that children who were displaced by public housing demolitions and given housing vouchers to move to less disadvantaged neighborhoods were 9 percent more likely to be employed as adults than their nondisplaced peers and had 16 percent more in annual earnings than their peers.[21] This research suggests that children stand to benefit by living in areas with less income segregation.

Over the past few decades, the size of the Black middle and upper classes has undergone a sharp expansion. As these families have grown richer, as with whites, they have sought out newer, larger homes in neighborhoods with less crime and better-performing schools.[22] This has further isolated minority high-poverty neighborhoods in cities. In recent decades, many middle-class African Americans have suburbanized. William Julius Wilson has argued that an unintended consequence of the suburbanization of many African American families is that young people have less contact with role models.[23] If talented and ambitious people leave segregated urban areas, the young people there may underestimate the economic returns from learning skills because they do not have face-to-face contact with highly successful people.

To counter this trend, well-intentioned efforts have encouraged higher-income Blacks to live in poor Black neighborhoods. The Nehemiah homes in West Poplar, Philadelphia, are a well-known example.[24] This program, completed in the late 1990s, encouraged middle-class African Americans to purchase affordable new homes in some of the poorest areas of the city. According to surveys of the new homeowners, few brought children to the area, they owned cars and shopped in other parts of the city, and they built fences around their complexes.[25] This research suggests that little interaction was taking place between neighbors of different income groups.

Consequences for Minority Families and Children

Racial and income segregation have four broad effects. First, residential isolation limits labor market opportunities because of the spatial mismatch effect, as discussed in the previous chapter. Second, it limits African American asset portfolios. Third, it concentrates poor minority residents in areas with negative peer effects. Fourth, it results in less access to resources and an increased risk of negative health outcomes.

Given that real estate prices are higher in areas featuring higher quality of life, poor people are forced to concentrate in areas with lower quality of life. This has implications for the long-run achievement of children growing up in these neighborhoods, because positive peer effects, good schools, safe streets, and clean air are key inputs in growing up healthy and achieving one's full potential.

Given that many Black adults seek to own their own homes, a large number of Black homeowners own homes in Black areas. But home prices in these places have gone up relatively little or not at all over time. This means that such housing is affordable, but it has not been a good asset. Recent research has documented that African Americans who bought homes in the second half of the 20th century did not earn a high rate of return on this investment because they paid higher initial prices for the house, which then lost some of its original value once their white neighbors fled for the suburbs in response to their arrival.[26]

In 2016, the median Black household in the United States had less than 12 percent of the wealth of the median white household.[27] Although the two groups' incomes are more equal, Black households do not have comparable saved wealth, often inherited from previous generations, to fall back on in a period of hardship, to invest in future education, or to purchase valuable assets like houses. As a result, Black households cannot access bank loans and assume debt as easily as white households. The proliferation of establishments providing payday loans in communities of color attests to this. These loans with predatory terms, which are becoming increasingly accessible online, further trap families in poverty as the families attempt to deal with immediate financial crises.

The COVID-19 pandemic highlighted how minority neighborhoods are at greater risk for poor health outcomes. Death rates were significantly higher in majority-Black neighborhoods in our cities, revealing the existing vulnerabilities and the lack of access to health care and other resources to address public health concerns.

Residential Segregation and Negative Neighborhood and Peer Effects

A consequence of racial segregation within our cities is that poor families live in neighborhoods with the lowest quality of life, which typically feature high levels of crime and pollution and worse local public goods such as public schools. One measure of this effect is that Black residents of more segregated cities suffer from worse outcomes in education, employment, and single parenthood, even after controlling for their choices of where to live.[28]

The high homicide rates in our cities and in specific neighborhoods within our cities is one of the clearest indicators of the negative impacts of residential segregation. Rates of homicides per 100,000 residents in our cities in 2018 ranged from 18 in Pittsburgh to 61 in St. Louis, while the national rate was 6 (figure 5.3). Philadelphia, Cleveland, and Pittsburgh all have had significantly lower homicide rates in recent years than have Baltimore, Detroit, and St. Louis, but all these cities have higher rates than most

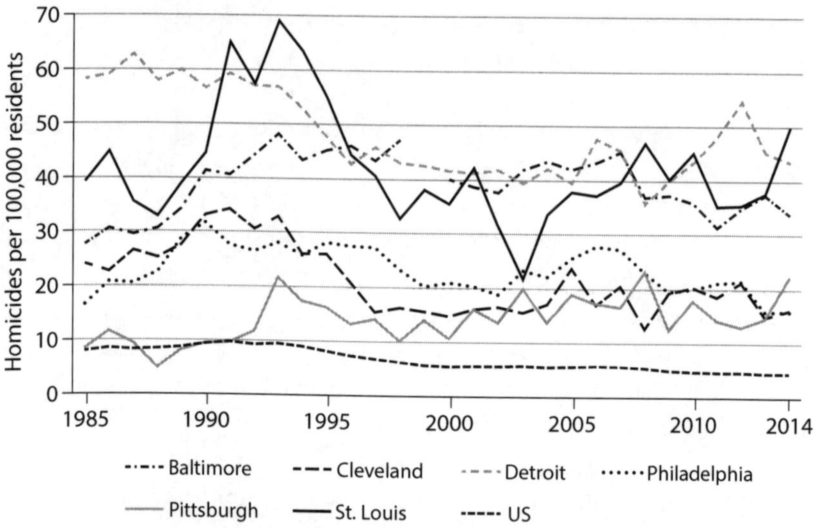

Figure 5.3. The number of homicides per 100,000 residents in the six cities are all well above the national average. Source: FBI Uniform Crime Reporting

major cities in the United States. The murder rate tends to be higher in cities with a greater share of African Americans. Within each city, the amount of violence varies by neighborhood. In Baltimore, for example, 11 zip codes had no murders in 2018, while zip code 21223 had 35 homicides and zip code 21217 had 48. The latter zip code's population is 85 percent Black.

While a decline in the homicide rate in Baltimore and Philadelphia from 2005 to 2014 might look promising, one need only look at more recent data to see troubling trends (figure 5.4). After declining in the early 2000s to 2014, the murder rate had a sharp increase in 2015. This increase is especially alarming given that the number of murders in New York City declined from 570 to 289 over these years, even as the numbers rose above 340 in Baltimore and Philadelphia. Similarly, the murder count in the City of Los Angeles was 258 in 2018, even though that city has almost seven times as many people as Baltimore City.

These observations beg the question of why crime declined in Baltimore and Philadelphia in the first place. Knowing that the drug trade is a major cause of violence in American cities, many police departments have focused on arresting drug dealers with the goal of reducing crime, but this has resulted in an unintended consequence. Counterintuitively, researchers found

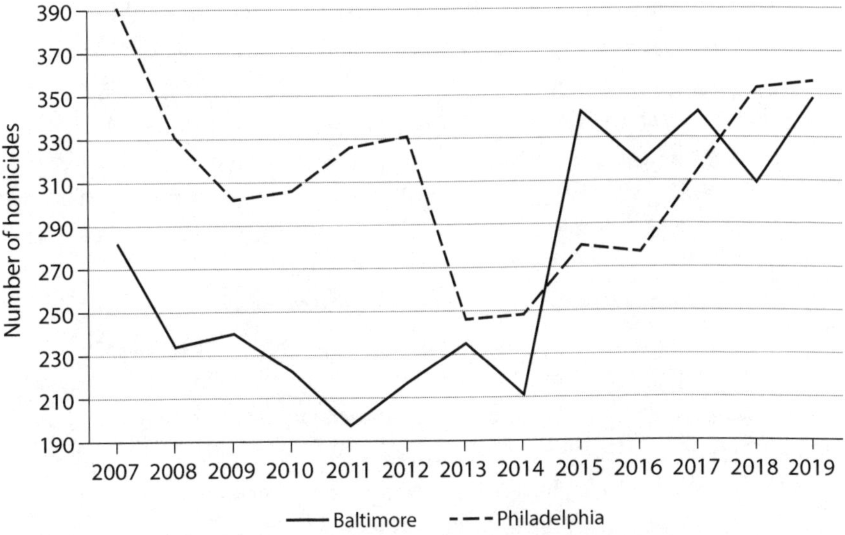

Figure 5.4. The total number of homicides in Baltimore and Philadelphia dropped from 2006 through 2014 but then rose.

that surges in arrests for illegal drug dealing actually led to more gun violence over the long term given the high demand for illegal drugs.[29] Arresting drug dealers created a power vacuum in which other dealers fought over the right to deal in the newly opened territory, leading to an increase in shootings and homicides. In contrast, researchers found the most significant positive effects for interventions that targeted possession of an illegal weapon. However, given the federal indictments brought against Baltimore City's Gun Trace Task Force, these specialized units require an intense level of oversight if they are to be effective.

A 2017 Temple University study found that Philadelphia's CeaseFire program was associated with a reduction in shootings of 30 percent in target neighborhoods. Like Safe Streets Baltimore, CeaseFire is modeled on Chicago's Cure Violence program, which uses violence "interrupters" to stop the spread of gun violence by targeting high-risk places and people.[30] These programs set up centers in the hardest-hit communities in their respective cities. They then use credible violence interrupters, who are usually people who used to deal drugs or be involved in violent crime themselves, to go to corners where the violence is taking place and mediate disputes. The interrupters have the local knowledge and reputation to calm escalating conflicts on the street, whereas a police officer or other social servant might not. The city also used focused deterrence from 2013 to 2017 and credited it with a 35 percent reduction in shootings. After the strategy was abandoned in 2018, homicides rose sharply.[31] Baltimore City experienced similar success with a strategy of focused deterrence under Sheila Dixon's mayoral administration. However, the strategy was also abandoned in the years after corruption charges caused Mayor Dixon to resign.[32]

The Consequences of Exposure to Violence

That some African American neighborhoods feature greater levels of violence has implications for multiple generations. In Baltimore, an estimated 80 percent of children have experienced violence in their neighborhood. This and other adverse childhood experiences, such as witnessing domestic violence or experiencing parental substance abuse or incarceration, take a mental and physical toll on the well-being of children. Researchers are only beginning to understand the full extent of these negative experiences on later life outcomes. For example, recent research has highlighted how students are more likely to be absent from school if their commute includes traveling through areas with high rates of violent crimes.[33]

The perception that African American neighborhoods are high-crime neighborhoods acts as a "tax" on African American parts of the city. If richer people believe these areas are unsafe, they will be less likely to spend time there, which reduces the demand for local services provided by businesspeople and lowers their profits. Such a "separate and unequal" mindset means that certain neighborhoods in our six cities have become increasingly isolated from the rest of the city.

Children are more racially segregated by neighborhood than adults, as levels of neighborhood segregation among families with children is about twice as high as it is for families without children.[34] This has a direct effect on public school segregation. Public school classrooms in our cities are not integrated along racial or income lines. The children of wealthy and educated parents are unlikely to attend these schools. From 1987 to 2016, the share of Black students enrolled in city schools remained relatively the same as white students were mostly replaced by Hispanic students (figure 5.5). The number of white students attending public schools in each of our cities declined significantly, as did their share of the school district population, reaching as little as 2 percent in the City of Detroit's school district.[35]

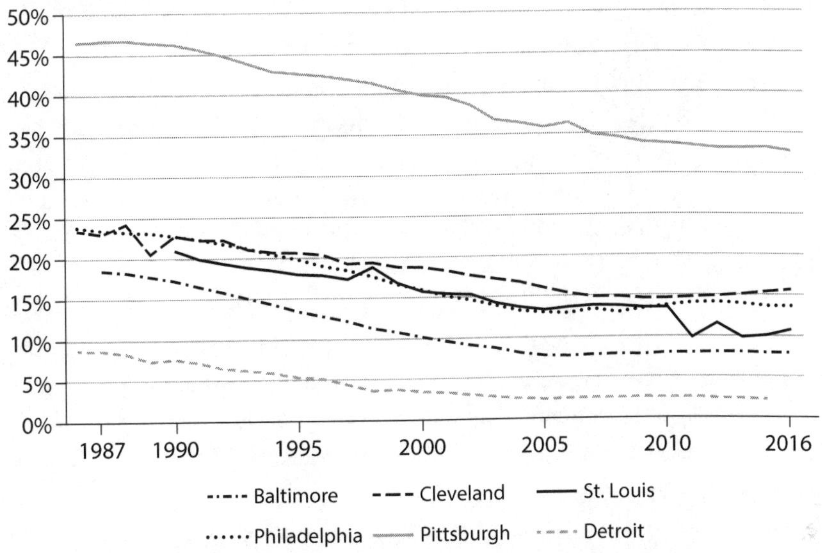

Figure 5.5. The percentage of white students enrolled in the public school systems of the six cities has dropped since 1987, with a slight rise in more recent years. Source: Urban Institute Education Data Explorer

Rucker Johnson has argued that school segregation has important implications for children of all races.[36] African Americans who attend integrated schools demonstrate dramatic improvements in educational attainment, earnings, and health status. The longer students attended well-funded, integrated schools, "the better their outcomes in adulthood."[37]

Environmental Justice Disparities

Poor minority city dwellers often live in the oldest housing in the poorest parts of cities. These structures expose children to higher levels of lead, a toxin with neurological effects. Childhood lead exposure affects the development of the prefrontal cortex and is associated with a decrease in cognitive abilities and executive functioning. Exposure to lead can lower children's IQ and increase the chances they will suffer from attention deficit disorder. The exposure of many children to high levels of lead creates a social environment prone to violence. Research found that a sharp reduction in childhood lead exposure reported at the state level in the 1970s and 1980s was partly responsible for a reduction in violent crime in the

1990s.[38] However, exposure levels remain high, especially in communities with older housing stock and exposed soil in vacant lots. A study in Milwaukee found that the share of firearm violence attributable to elevated blood lead levels was 56 percent for perpetration and 51 percent for victimization for children born between 1986 and 2003.[39] Minority children are also exposed to more noxious industrial sites and higher particulate levels, which creates a differential in air pollution exposure for whites and minorities.[40]

Recent research has used linked administrative records to document the long-run labor market consequences of growing up in a more polluted environment. This research has demonstrated, for example, that a baby's exposure to toxic industrial plants during gestation can lead to worse labor market outcomes, more poverty, less education, and disabilities in adulthood.[41]

Given the challenges that they face, the children of poor people who grow up in these polluted places are also at great risk of being poor. Living in high-poverty areas has intergenerational implications.[42] Remediating or mitigating these environmental hazards could have a large effect on improving outcomes for poor people, thereby improving the quality of life in these neighborhoods.

Residential Segregation's Implications for Distrust across Groups

In the six cities, African Americans tend to live in areas that are mainly Black, while whites tend to live in predominantly white areas. Since we spend much of our time close to where we live, this means that the two groups seldom interact in their neighborhoods. And if many young African Americans are not working, the two groups have few opportunities for interacting at work either. As a result, stereotypes and mistrust about the two groups persist because members of one group are largely strangers to the other.

The absence of "bridging" social capital between racial groups in these cities has implications for urban politics, collective action, school segregation, and employment. If whites politically support a program or issue, concerns tend to arise about whether the program will be good for Blacks. This mentality of a zero-sum game contributes to mistrust and injures an urban democracy. In cities like Baltimore, leading institutions like Johns Hopkins

University have engaged in activities that have injured the Black community. The ability of such institutions to make significant investments that will result in shared prosperity hinges on building trust and finding common goals.

Recent research from the Brookings Institution found that businesses located in majority-Black neighborhoods received fewer Yelp online reviews than did businesses in white neighborhoods, after controlling for consumer wealth, consumer growth, and consumer proximity.[43] The researchers also found that the businesses receiving higher ratings or a larger number of reviews experienced faster revenue growth. This study has important implications for both consumers and business owners in segregated neighborhoods. In majority-Black neighborhoods, business quality tends to be less related to performance, so poorly rated businesses are able to compete with highly rated ones. Similarly, for owners, providing high-quality customer service and products does not necessarily result in financial rewards in Black neighborhoods.

Several of our cities have experienced riots in recent decades, as exemplifed by the unrest set off by Freddie Gray's death in Baltimore in April 2015.[44] Urban economists have argued that the probability of an urban riot is higher in areas with less bridging social capital across different groups. One study of real estate prices in cities concluded that the racial gap in the value of real estate widened over time in cities that experienced race riots in the 1960s. This finding might be explained by a fear of recurrence: the demand by richer people to live in Black neighborhoods declines in the aftermath of riots because some of them fear such salient events will recur. Persistent fear acts as a tax on social interactions across income and racial lines. If different income groups and different racial groups do not interact, then trust, mutual respect, and understanding are less likely to develop.

The "Goldilocks" Effect: Balancing the Benefits of Gentrification while Avoiding Displacement

The cities of Washington, DC, and New York City have experienced significant crime reduction, which has unleashed both the costs and benefits of gentrification as richer people have sought to visit and live in areas that they shunned in the past. From the perspective of urban economics, the challenge is that we are not able to run a controlled experiment in which we can reduce neighborhood crime and then observe the effects. We instead must rely on natural experiments to help us understand how cities and their neighborhoods are affected by declining crime.

When crime declines in neighborhoods with strong fundamentals (such as proximity to great parts of the city), local demand for housing and rents will rise. This effect is especially pronounced when local zoning codes make it difficult for developers to build new housing. In this case, as rents rise, local homeowners enjoy a financial windfall from rising rents, but renters already living there may be priced out of their neighborhood. Similarly, local homeowners may not be able to pay the increased taxes on their property and may be forced to sell and move out. In this way, urban progress introduces distributional effects that hinge on the initial property ownership of local assets.

When a neighborhood's quality of life improves, local housing demand increases. Whether increases in demand translate into sharp increases in local rents hinges on the supply of housing. In recent years, a major research topic in urban and real estate economics has been the limits to new housing supply. If real estate developers face high costs due to the topography of the land or local zoning regulation, the supply curve of local housing will be almost vertical. An inability to build new housing creates signficant issues for gentrification.[45]

When developers cannot tear down existing single-family structures and erect larger multi-family apartment buildings, increases in local housing demand will lead to soaring rents. In the booming cities of Boston, Portland, Seattle, and San Francisco, this phenomenon has played out again and again, with thousands of residents being displaced. However, our cities feature vacant land on which to build, and we are confident that builders can engage in infill development if regulations do not limit such new construction. The net effect of new housing supply is to temper concerns about soaring rents.

Most neighborhoods in our cities are not under an immediate threat of gentrification and displacement of current residents. However, from Cass Corridor and downtown in Detroit to Remington and the Inner Harbor in Baltimore to Uptown in Cleveland, several neighborhoods have gentrified, thus displacing neighborhood residents. These trends are most concerning in Philadelphia and Pittsburgh, which have seen more widespread gentrification. Rent.com calculated that rental price increases in Philadelphia for one-bedroom apartments from 2018 to 2019 were 28 percent in Northern Liberties, 17 percent in Burholme, and 13 percent in University City and

Rittenhouse Square. Pittsburgh experienced annual rental price increases of 10 percent in North Side, 8 percent in North Shore, and 7 percent in Allegheny Center. A recent report by the Abell Foundation found that the in-migration of young, wealthy whites in Baltimore City corresponded with the gentrification of half of the predominantly white tracts in the city that were at risk of gentrification in 2000. The same effect was found for only a small number of majority-Black tracts, which were more likely to see population loss than gentrification.[46]

When cities do nothing to safeguard neighborhoods against gentrification and displacement, inaction can lead to contentious relationships between newcomers and longtime residents. This antagonism often has a racial or class component as wealthier white residents move into neighborhoods, drive up rents, and change the cultural and commercial landscape of the neighborhood with boutique stores and coffee shops offering retail and services that longtime residents cannot afford or do not want. While gentrification can improve the economic prospects of a neighborhood, it can also cause deep divides among people living in the same city by deteriorating the social fabric.

Another strategy to protect poor residents against rising rents is the creation of a community land trust. The six cities we study currently have a large number of city-owned vacant properties and land parcels. The city government could transfer all of these parcels to a community land trust that would be community owned and held as a portfolio of assets similar to a real estate investment trust. Members of the trust would be longtime city residents who are renters or homeowners living below the poverty line. The trust could rent the land to private businesses or sell land parcels as a neighborhood's value rises. Profits could be reinvested or distributed to members as a lump sum, similar to the Alaska Permanent Fund. Members could use the income to invest in education, purchase a home, or start up a business. The creation of this type of trust would serve two primary purposes. First, it would protect poor renters and homeowners against gentrification and ensure that they financially benefit from it. Second, it would create a "stakeholder society" where poor residents have a stake and thus a real incentive to promote economic growth in their city.[47] Members of the trust would then be able to profit in their city's comeback.

Setting the Stage

The evidence presented in the preceding four chapters suggests that these six cities are at an important juncture. A great city features people investing in their own skills and investing in assets that they own in their neighborhoods. Conversely, a weak city features underinvestment in both people and places. Many of the residents of these cities are caught in a poverty trap.[48] If families, real estate investors, and businesses expect that a given city is in decline, each of them will reduce their investments in it. Children in school will devote less attention to learning. Real estate investors will allow properties to deteriorate rather than renovating or upgrading them. Businesses will be less likely to pursue ambitious expansion goals. As each of these individual urban investors makes these choices to withhold or divest, the city's overall well-being flounders.

Despite all the descriptive research about urban poverty, we still do not know the "formula" for eliminating poverty. At a time when technological optimists celebrate the power of algorithms for predicting what Netflix videos people will like or choosing the right date for a single person, we do not have a predictive algorithm for helping people escape poverty. The research frontier is complicated by the fact that copious data are required to understand how children born poor in one of our cities could grow up to achieve the American Dream. A multitude of factors enter into this success equation, including the roles of parents, peers, schools, stress, pollution, crime, transit, housing, and many other urban factors. What has to go right to escape poverty?

As optimists, we foresee a pathway for iteratively learning about which family, neighborhood, and citywide conditions can maximize the probability that young people will achieve their full potential. Economic growth relieves us of the logic of a zero-sum game. In a growing economy, one person's gain does not have to come at the expense of another's loss. For poverty rates to decline sharply in these cities, economic growth must accelerate. This economic growth is unlikely to come from a major expansion of the public sector. The private sector must choose of its own volition to invest in these places.

Local governments play a crucial role in setting priorities to spur private-sector investments in people and places. Elected officials, and the voters who put them in decision-making seats of power, ultimately decide on the set of policies for and investments in places and people that local governments then implement. These policies can either enable economic mobility and opportunity or restrict the ability of children to reach their full potential. In chapter six, we explore the urban politics. Do elected officials in our six cities have the right incentives to craft policies and make strategic investments that will improve the quality of life in their cities, while offering economic upward mobility to families living in poverty? Chapter six explores this question by examining both the manner in which elected officials come to and stay in power and the most crucial policy areas they oversee.

NOTES

1. Baum-Snow 2007.
2. Dingel and Neiman 2020.
3. Alon, Doepke, Olmstead-Rumsey, and Tertilt 2020.
4. Costa and Kahn 2000.
5. Hirschman 1970.
6. Lazear 2001.
7. Reardon and Bischoff 2016.
8. Baltimore City Health Department 2011.
9. Cutler, Glaeser, and Vigdor 1999.
10. Boustan 2016.
11. Derenoncourt 2019.
12. Pietila 2010.
13. Conklin, Ambrose, and Lopez 2019.
14. Brinkman and Lin 2019.
15. Christensen and Timmins 2018.
16. Bayer, Fang, and McMillan 2014; Waldfogel 2008; Olsen 2014; Schelling 1972; Card, Mas, and Rothstein 2008.
17. Goodman 2018.
18. Howell 2018.
19. Chyn 2018; Jacob, Ludwig, and Miller 2013.
20. Carter, Schill, and Wachter 1998.
21. Chyn 2018.
22. Margo 1992.
23. Wilson 2008, 2012; Jensen 2010.
24. Cummings, DiPasquale, and Kahn 2002.
25. US Department of Housing and Urban Development 2011.
26. Akbar, Li, Shertzer, and Walsh 2019.
27. Kuhn, Schularick, and Steins 2018.
28. Cutler and Glaeser 1997.
29. Webster, Buggs, and Crifasi 2018.
30. Roman, Klein, Wolff, Bellamy, and Reeves 2017.
31. Loeb 2019.
32. Meyer 2020.
33. Burdick-Will, Stein, and Grigg 2019.
34. Jargowsky 2014.
35. Urban Institute.
36. Johnson 2019.
37. Strauss 2019.
38. Reyes 2007.
39. Emer, Kalkbrenner, O'Brien, Yan, Cisler, and Weinhardt 2020.
40. Christensen, Sarmiento-Barbieri, and Timmins 2020.
41. Persico 2020.
42. Chetty and Hendren 2018.
43. Perry, Rothwell, and Harshbarger 2020.
44. DiPasquale and Glaeser 1998; Collins and Margo 2007.
45. Saiz 2010; Glaeser and Gyourko 2005; Glaeser, Gyourko, and Saks 2005.
46. Mallach 2020.
47. Ackerman and Alstott 1999.
48. Durlauf 2012; Durlauf and Ioannides 2010.

6

Improving Urban Governance

Richard M. Daley served as the mayor of Chicago from 1989 to 2011. During that time, Chicago's economy, quality of life, and real estate prices all grew, and Mr. Daley was reelected five times, ultimately becoming the city's longest-running mayor after declining to run for a seventh term.

Chicago's success during Mayor Daley's years of service raises several questions about urban governance. How much of Chicago's success during that period was due to his leadership? Did his policies and government hires contribute directly to Chicago's success? Or is he lucky that he now receives a lot of credit for a boom that would have taken place even if he hadn't been mayor?

The challenge in evaluating the effects of leadership is constructing the "what if" (or, in the language of economics, the "counterfactual"). What would Chicago's economic and quality of life dynamics have been from 1989 to 2011 if Daley had not been mayor? Since we do not have a twin for Chicago, it is difficult to evaluate the value added of any urban leader.

The same issue arises in evaluating the effectiveness of corporate leaders. Researchers have studied whether chief executive officers (CEOs) were compensated for being lucky or whether their pay was tied to their actual performance. By looking at observable measures of improvement in the business cycle outside a CEO's control, such as large increases in oil prices, the researchers found that CEO pay is as much tied to luck as it is to performance.[1]

This chapter explores urban political power and the role it plays in shaping the economy and quality of life in our six cities. Their mayors face significant governance challenges as they allocate a tight budget across many areas, including education, housing, safety, parks, cultural institutions, transit, and infrastructure maintenance and upgrades. While mayors in different cities have different powers, each of them must decide how to handle crime, public school investment, economic growth initiatives, and budget balancing by setting taxes and negotiating with public-sector unions.

Public-Sector Unions

An emerging urban economics literature has examined how public-sector unions both raise the cost of public-service delivery and reduce experimentation as these entities seek to protect their members.[2] As demonstrated by the enormous popularity of Uber and ride sharing, urban innovation in service delivery does involve disruption. A fear of the side effects (such as job loss) induced by innovation can lead to stagnation and an inferior quality of services. Given that many people in our cities rely on the state for health, transport, schooling, trash collection, street safety, and other services, it is essential that these cities consider new strategies to raise the quality of these services. If public-sector unions focus on minimizing job loss and maximizing pay for union members, labor contracts are unlikely to focus on the quality of local service delivery.

Police unions have come under increased scrutiny and criticism after officers of the Minneapolis Police Department killed George Floyd on May 26, 2020. Baltimore City is an extreme example of how police union protections can stand in the way of change. Maryland's Law Enforcement Officers' Bill of Rights, passed in the 1970s, provides broad protections for police officers from being prosecuted for on-the-job misconduct and prevents public oversight and scrutiny of police. Information on public complaints and disciplinary records are exempt from disclosure under the Maryland Public Information Act. When a police officer is accused of misconduct, the department undertakes an internal review, and the process and result are hidden from the public, with the department ultimately having all decision-making power. While the Civilian Review Board of Baltimore City exists, it is largely toothless.[3] The protections afforded by the legislation make it almost impossible for the public and elected officials to get rid of so-called bad apples in the police department and make many reforms impossible.

Embracing a Culture of Experimentation

Our cities feature many leaders who have spent their careers in city government. These career profiles raise questions about whether they have sufficient knowledge and trust of the private sector. Mayor Michael R. Bloomberg's fluid transition from the private sector to becoming the mayor of New York City and back to the private sector is rare. Have our six cities experienced enough creative "disruption" as new leaders have infused city hall with new ideas? Mayors tend to have a short time horizon, as they expect to serve for four or eight years before they leave office or lose an election. The residents of a city, in contrast, typically hope that a mayor will make investments that may involve short-term costs yet also provide long-term gains.

No known "one size fits all" policy can guarantee urban economic growth while simultaneously improving the quality of life for the poor and attracting skilled workers to a city. Given this fact, it is crucial for mayors to create a culture of experimentation and ex post evaluation to learn "what works." Mayor Bloomberg embraced this iterative scientific approach. Under his leadership, several data metrics were created to measure in real time what challenges were arising in different New York City neighborhoods.[4]

This experimental culture does not exist in every city. In many of our cities, a business-as-usual mentality reigns. Our cities are constantly struggling to "put out fires." City leaders and agency heads can underinvest in time spent on long-term planning because they are rushing from one emergency to the next. Each of our cities' mayors faces the challenge of meeting the needs of a large number of poor people. At the same time, each center city competes with its suburbs and other center cities to attract footloose and skilled people and firms. Cities also need to build talent and wealth from within, by investing in education and building up neighborhoods. If cities cannot retain and attract the footloose and build wealth from within, the tax base will not grow, and no new revenue will be available to help the poor.

Encouraging Civic Participation

In the 2017 mayoral Democratic primary in Pittsburgh, incumbent Bill Peduto won the nomination with 27,270 votes. He ran unopposed in the general election, meaning that 27,270, or 9 percent, of the total population of Pittsburgh had effectively decided who the next mayor would be. In winning her 2017 mayoral election, Lyda Krewson received just 17,110 votes in the Democratic primary for St. Louis, a city of 320,000 people, meaning that merely 5 percent of the population chose the new mayor in a city that has not seen a Republican mayor since 1949.

Mayoral candidates are aware that few people vote and that a relatively small number of voters can decide elections. They therefore have an incentive to focus their efforts on those pockets of the city with supportive voters and cater to their interests. Poor people in poor parts of these cities are less likely to vote. This effectively disenfranchises them, since a mayor seeking reelection has less of an incentive to prioritize helping them. Black voters are even less likely to turn out to vote. Political scientist and Baltimore City Council member John Bullock posits the following in the context of Baltimore: "I think [the low turnout] has to do with the conditions that people have lived under for a number of years," he said. "They may look at their neighborhoods, their schools and public services, and [they may] not see much of a change whether they vote or not. So they figure, 'Well, why vote anyway?'"[5]

Individual voters have little incentive to invest their time in becoming informed about how the different candidates approach key issues because such effort is costly and any one vote will not be pivotal in the election. Given low turnout, local interest groups can exercise significant power. Their donations fund targeted media campaigns on television, radio, and social media. While we do not fully understand the role that this money plays in affecting the outcomes of local elections, the ongoing questions about Facebook's role in the 2016 presidential election highlights the importance of understanding what sways the people who actually do vote.[6]

Each of our cities has not had a Republican mayor in decades. Given this fact, the Democratic primary often decides who will become mayor in our six cities. In 2016, Baltimore City had roughly 610,000 people. Of these, 296,256 were registered voters. During that year's Democratic primary, 133,171 turned out to vote. Of these, 48,709 voted for Catherine Pugh, who ultimately became the next mayor. This means that around 8 percent of the city's population effectively decided who the next mayor would be. This is a very small mandate.

Given that most people in our cities do not vote in local elections, what policies and practices could encourage higher voter turnout and civic participation? Nobel laureate economist Eric Maskin is a proponent of ranked-choice voting, which lets a voter vote for multiple candidates by ranking them in order of the voter's preference.[7] Cities and states across the United States have adopted it to encourage voter turnout and to give citizens an increased sense of participation in the democratic process because their vote matters more. As we discussed above, one of the potential reasons for low voter turnout is a belief that nothing will really change. If our cities gave their electorate the opportunity to have more of a say in what happens in the governance of their communities, would residents be more likely to vote?

While open-data portals have allowed urban residents to measure the effectiveness of their governments and increase accountability, the data do not offer a direct way to engage in politics. Recognizing that most people are not data-savvy analysts, the Baltimore Neighborhood Indicators Alliance at the University of Baltimore publishes annual reports on the health and progress of local communities. The organization then invites members of the community and local leaders to discuss the findings and think about how they can use them to signal priorities to local government.

In Paris, France, voters have a say in how the local government spends 5 percent of its annual budget through a participatory budgeting practice where residents propose ideas for using the funds and then vote on them. The goal of this practice is greater collaboration between government and the people it serves. Would implementing a similar type of participatory budgeting in our cities increase the public's trust in government and lead to greater voter turnout?

An alternative approach is taken by the organization Cities of Service, which, through its Love Your Block program, provides local governments with funds to disburse to residents for revitalizing their block. By providing people in the community with the funding and know-how to improve their neighborhood, the organization hopes to drive greater civic participation and a feeling of connection to city hall. Whether this actually results in a more engaged citizenry remains an open question.

What is clear is that our cities need to do a better job of working with communities and making residents believe that they not only have a voice but also that municipal policies and interventions are community based and oriented. If residents do not see the change they want in their neighborhood, they can ultimately vote with their feet.

The mayoral landscape of our cities is obviously important. Who chooses to run for mayor of these cities? What issues do those elected choose to prioritize? What power do they have? What special-interest groups are they beholden to? And what policy levers can mayors pull to strengthen their local economies and improve the quality of life.

Urban Mayor Career Trajectories

Certain insights can be gained by looking at the backgrounds of the six mayors who served in each of our cities in 2020. During the previous 10 years, Baltimore had seven mayors. Political scandal caused several of these mayors to resign from office, including Sheila Dixon in 2010 and Catherine Pugh in 2019. Bernard C. "Jack" Young became the mayor of Baltimore City on May 2, 2019. He had served from 2010 to 2019 as the president of the Baltimore City Council and, for 14 years prior to that, as a city council member. The majority of Mayor Young's career had been in public service, starting out as staff to a city council member in the late 1980s before going to work at the Maryland Department of Human Resources.

Mayor Frank Jackson had served as mayor of Cleveland since 2006. Like Mayor Young, Mayor Jackson spent the majority of his career in politics. Before his 14 years as mayor, which make him the second-longest-serving mayor in Cleveland's history, he started out as an assistant city prosecutor in the 1980s. Jackson became a city council member in 1989 and in 2001 was elected city council president.

In Detroit, Mike Duggan had served as mayor since 2014. His experience included positions in both the private and public sectors: he served as a deputy county executive in Wayne County in the 1980s and 1990s and as the president and CEO of the Detroit Medical Center for eight years, when he quit to run for mayor of Detroit.

In Philadelphia, Mayor Jim Kenney had been a longtime member of city hall, having been elected to the city council in 1991, when he was 32 years old. In Pittsburgh, voters elected William Peduto mayor in 2013. Prior to taking office, he had served for 19 years on the city council. Finally, Lyda Krewson had served as the mayor of St. Louis since 2017. From 1997 to 2017, she was alderman of St. Louis's 28th Ward.

A common theme across these mayors, with the exception of Mike Duggan, is a long career as a city public servant. Most had lived and worked in the city for their entire careers. While such institutional loyalty is admirable, these histories inevitably raise questions about a willingness and an appreciation for incorporating insights from the private sector and from other cities into city government. Insular thinking does not breed innovation.

The Interactions between Progressive Mayors and State and Federal Elected Officials

Political parties other than the Democratic Party play a small role in these cities. The last mayoral election in Pittsburgh featured no Republican candidate because nobody was able to get the 250 write-ins required to get on the ballot. In the last Philadelphia election, the Republican candidate received 19.4 percent of the vote.

Given that the Democratic Party candidate usually wins the election in the six cities, each state's governor and the US president have little political incentive to pay attention to these cities.[8] Self-interested state and federal officials focus their efforts on swaying swing voters. The residents of our six cities are not swing voters. Recognizing this point, Republican presidents have little incentive to invest federal dollars in these cities, and Republican governors know that they are taxing their base (suburbanites and rural voters) if they choose to help these cities through financial transfers.

After canceling state funding for the long-planned $2.9 billion light rail Red Line project in Baltimore City, Maryland governor Larry Hogan announced $2 billion in new road construction projects, none of which were located in the city. The COVID-19 pandemic highlighted Republican resistance to giving federal transfers to state and local governments, even in a time of extreme need, with Senate majority leader Mitch McConnell famously saying that he would rather see states go bankrupt than have the federal government intervene.[9] Given that the six cities receive relatively few state and federal transfers, they have a fiscal imperative to expand economic growth to create a more vibrant tax base.

In 2010, 10 percent of Baltimore's budget came from the federal government; by 2018, only 6 percent did. Given that our cities cannot expect large federal government interventions to solve their problems, they have to develop their own solutions and innovative policies. Bruce Katz and Jeremy Nowak argue this point in their recent book *The New Localism*, positing that power has devolved from national and state governments to local governments.[10]

The Objectives of Local Elected Officials

Elected officials enact urban policies with an eye toward how this shapes the local electorate. One troubling hypothesis in the urban political economy literature is known as the Curley effect, which is named for Boston mayor James Curley, who served from 1946 to 1950. The Curley effect posits that some mayors intentionally choose policies that cater to one group of voters (in Curley's case, Irish immigrants) while going against the interest of other groups. By pursuing such strategies, mobile voters who do not support the incumbent leave the jurisdiction. The net effect is a composition shift such that the incumbent mayor has an even larger probability of being reelected because the remaining voters are "his people." If the Curley effect holds, some mayors may sacrifice objective improvements in their city's economy and quality of life in order to improve their chances for reelection.

City residents who feel that their mayor does not champion their priorities always have the option of moving to the suburbs. They will contribute less in tax dollars to local governments. In Baltimore City, only 18 percent of the city's police force live in the city. Of Black police officers, only 22 percent live in the city.[11] If all 2,180 police officers had lived in Baltimore City in 2018, then 1,790 more officers would have contributed to city coffers. Median pay for a police officer was around $100,000 in 2018. So if those 1,790 officers owned homes with an average value of $200,000 (with a 1.7 percent rate of property tax) and paid income taxes to the city (at a 3.2 percent rate for a married filer), then Baltimore City would have seen around $11 million in additional revenue for that year. This is a conservative estimate and does not include increased local spending on entertainment and purchases at local stores and other positive spillover effects. In the current state of things, the majority of these officers live in the surrounding suburban counties and contribute to their tax bases.

Many elected positions in local government are not considered full-time jobs. This leads to some city council members being much more involved in the political process than others. For example, in Baltimore City, some city council members missed more than 50 percent of their committee votes, with an average of 25 percent of missed committee votes. Would these elected officials be more likely to show up for work if their position was a full-time job? Are longtime incumbents less likely to show up for votes because they feel secure in their position?

As mentioned above, elected officials often have a short time horizon of four to eight years before they expect to be out of office or running for a higher government office. This means that they will be more likely to adopt policies that show success in the short term and possibly not the long term. This serves as a barrier to adopting policies that make long-term investments in the well-being of people and neighborhoods in their cities. It also serves as a disincentive to admit failure. Elected officials prefer to tout their successes in office rather than discuss lessons they have learned from policies that did not turn out the way they had anticipated. This means they will be less likely to end a program they originally sponsored, as doing that would mean admitting that their idea did not prove successful. Such inadmission or even dishonesty inhibits learning and a culture of innovation and experimentation that could ultimately lead to more improvement and better policy.

Barriers to Innovation in Policy

Urban governments do not operate in a vacuum. As stated above, our cities cannot expect large transfers from state and federal governments, and in some cases, these have been declining. State government preemption of local and especially urban government policy making is a growing national trend that serves as a barrier to innovation. An example of state preemption is the North Carolina "bathroom bill" that prohibits transgender individuals from using multiple-occupancy public restrooms. Johns Hopkins public health researchers Lainie Rutkow and Jon Vernick conducted a national survey of mayors and public health officials and found that nearly all respondents found preemption to be an obstacle to local policy making.[12] When faced with preemption, 60 to 70 percent of officials either abandoned or delayed local policy-making efforts. The National League of Cities found that states have prevented cities from implementing policies on everything from ride sharing to municipal broadband to home sharing to tax and expenditure limitations.[13] These legal challenges from the state and occasionally the federal level inhibit the progress that cities can make in testing new ideas.

Furthermore, cities do not have control over many crucial policy issues. For example, in Baltimore City, the State of Maryland controls most of the levers of urban transportation dynamics through the Maryland Transit Administration, which controls the buses and passenger rail in the city.

Another example in Baltimore is the Baltimore City Public School System. The mayor controls appointments to the school board, which in turn controls the hiring and firing of the chief executive officer who runs the school system, but the mayor does not have control over how the school system is funded. That is determined at the state level. The city can and does contribute funding above and beyond what the state provides, but city officials do not have full control over how much money is spent on education. The city must lobby the state to affect that legislation.

Would city governments be more innovative than state governments if they controlled more of the determinants of local success? Would they be more likely to invest in things like rail and bus system improvements? An alternative hypothesis has it that more direct voter control could improve outcomes.[14]

Edward Glaeser argues that urban governments focus too much on limiting change and not enough on improving the urban experience.[15] He notes that the costs to entry for low-skill entrepreneurs are often much higher than for high-skill entrepreneurs. The public sector imposes fines and fees for bad behavior but often avoids making the environmental and systemic changes that would make such rule breaking unattractive or unnecessary. Immobility and sluggish decision-making by local governments limit the potential of urban residents and firms.

Binding Budget Constraints

The budgets of the six cities we study ranged from around $600 million a year in Pittsburgh to almost $5 billion a year in Philadelphia in 2020. While by no means small, these budgets must cover a variety of priorities that include health and public safety, transportation, economic development, parks and recreation, housing, water and sewer infrastructure, and servicing debt and pension liabilities. At the same time, these expenditures must satisfy a diverse group of constituents with varying needs and strong opinions about what their tax dollars should fund first. Allocating scarce resources to meet all of these needs seems like a daunting task.

A method that Baltimore adopted in the past decade is called "budgeting for outcomes." Baltimore City's budget director Andrew Kleine adopted the method during the depth of the 2008 recession with the goal of maximizing the impact of the city's scarce resources to help maintain a solid financial footing while meeting clearly defined, data-based goals centered on the mayoral administration's "priority outcomes and indicators."[16] For example, Baltimore's 2019 adopted budget includes "quality of life" as one of five major "priority outcomes" and lists the following services under quality of life: recycling rate, citywide energy use, water cleanliness, recreational opportunities, blight elimination, and childhood asthma. These are "services that are high-performing and closely aligned with the City's strategic goals."[17] The budget report goes on to list key indicators for evaluating each of these services and identifies both positive and negative factors the city will address in an effort to improve outcomes.

A particular challenge facing our six cities, and any other city that has experienced population decline in recent years, is the legacy of funding pensions for a larger government than what exists today. Recognizing the financial risk of having a large, unfunded pension liability, Baltimore City restructured its pension system in 2010, which led to a reduction in the unfunded pension liability from $3.1 billion to $2.6 billion. However, the legacy of a larger government remains, most clearly seen in the city's Fire and Police Employees' Retirement System pension in recent years. As the number of active duty police officers fell from 2010 to 2019 and the number of retirees increased, the ratio of inactive retirees benefiting from the system to active employees paying into the pension system increased from 1.31 in 2010 to 1.59 in 2019. Over the same time, the city's contribution rate grew from around 30 percent to almost 50 percent. In the late 1990s, the value of assets in the pension fund was above the liability, but it declined from 104 percent of the liability to just 70 percent by 2019.[18]

This example highlights how even fiscally responsible governments that reduce spending and prioritize outcomes during market downturns may still have to account for the historical legacy of a government that provided services to thousands more residents than that government does today. With this in mind, local governments in post-industrial cities must prioritize both outcomes-based budgeting and economic growth to ensure that they are able to cover costs. We use this logic in the following sections by considering several important policy areas relevant to the quality of life in the six cities.

Urban Peer Learning Networks

In 2019, Baltimore City launched the Lots to Love pilot program, which targeted 47 vacant lots for maintenance and care. The program was modeled after Philadelphia's LandCare program and was adopted after a study had assessed the randomized trial program and found that it significantly reduced violent crime and increased use of outside space for recreation.[19] In 2019, Baltimore City hosted its sister city Rotterdam, the Netherlands, for a flood resilience conference where Baltimore could learn from Rotterdam's internationally praised success for living with water. These interactions demonstrate the value of peer learning but occur on an ad hoc basis.

Ideally, leaders of similar types of cities (e.g., post-industrial cities) would interact with each other regularly through a formal process to learn valuable new strategies that peer cities have recently piloted. Such knowledge consortiums require coordination that foundations could help facilitate. The Rockefeller Foundation's 100 Resilient Cities represents just one example of such learning networks. A self-selection issue arises. The mayors who are most curious about learning what works, and who are most eager to try out ideas that have shown themselves to be promising in another city, will be the ones who sign up for such networks. Unfortunately, it is the cities whose mayors do not show open-minded interest in initiatives like this that are likely to benefit the most from joining such an effort. Urban-focused foundations could use their grant-making clout to nudge urban mayors to participate in such learning networks. The Nobel laureate Paul Romer maintains that once a promising policy idea has been piloted and an ex post evaluation indicates that it has been effective, this policy can then be tried out in other cities to see if it results in similar benefits. The key here is curiosity among city officials and an understanding of which other cities are close peers. If a new policy works in Philadelphia, we can presume little about how it might benefit a small town in rural Texas, but a Baltimore City official might be more confident that it would demonstrate similar results in Baltimore.

Fostering Urban Economic Growth

Since no one recipe guarantees local economic growth, local mayors can justify many different strategies for pursuing this worthy goal.[20] Urban economists argue that a city's human capital level is the most important determinant of economic growth. At any point in time, a city can increase its stock of human capital by investing in its own current residents (both youths and adults) or by recruiting new entrants to the city. One challenge, though, with increasing local human capital is that people, once trained, can move away. The University of Michigan has wrestled with this issue as the taxpayers of Michigan have asked why they are paying taxes to subsidize the education of students at the University of Michigan when many of them move to California after graduation. A city featuring a well-trained workforce must continue to offer great quality of life to retain these people and to attract newcomers. Facing finite budgets, decision makers seeking to stimulate growth must choose between how much to invest in the skills of urban people versus investing in urban places.

State efforts to create high-quality public universities represent one human-capital investment strategy. Another is to invest in increasing the population's geographic mobility. The poor face a small menu of affordable geographic options. That is why Moving to Opportunity, a family-based program of the Department of Housing and Urban Development, seeks to help low-income families move to higher-income neighborhoods. But how do these voucher recipients choose where to move, and how does their relocation to a new area affect the quality of life where they end up and where they left? In this game of musical chairs, who replaces them and whom do they replace?[21]

Cities in the South often argue that the key to their place-based growth strategy is low taxes and light regulation. Given that the mayors of our cities are Democrats, few are likely to pursue a low-tax strategy for generating economic activity. States such as Florida feature no state income tax. California has mild weather and high taxes on the wealthy, with a state tax rate for the richest residents of 13.5 percent. Rich people are willing to stay and pay such taxes when they are compensated with a great quality of life. But a high-tax, low-service city will not attract firms and will lose its tax base to the suburbs or to other metro areas. Economists have documented that cities with high taxes relative to their level of services feature lower home prices. The market punishes property owners in cities where residents are "overtaxed." This provides homeowners with an incentive to see that government officials provide high-quality services more efficiently, but few people in our cities vote in elections, and a handful of corporate interests and local public-sector unions are powerful in these cities.

Because our cities have a greater share of people living in poverty than the national average, city governments have to fund anti-poverty programs and provide a higher level of emergency services. State and federal governments largely do not compensate cities for such services, so the cities must bear the additional costs themselves.[22] In 1995, the City of Philadelphia spent $84 per capita on poverty-related services (excluding public hospitals), which was twice that of other cities. Larger cities have to spend a larger share of their revenues on poverty-related programs than smaller communities with lower poverty rates.[23]

Cities spend a significant amount of money in the form of incentives meant to attract firms. The average incentive is around $178 million for 1,500 promised jobs, at a cost of over $100,000 per job. While firms that receive these subsidies tend to produce the promised jobs, researchers have found no evidence of spillover benefits, suggesting that large gains could come from reforming these policies.[24] Economist Tim Bartik argues that these policies need to be more targeted to distressed places and redirected away from large firms toward cost-effective policies that demonstrate a lower cost per job.[25]

At the federal level, a variety of funding mechanisms exist with the goal of improving low- and moderate-income neighborhoods in cities. Community Development Block Grants, New Markets Tax Credits, Empowerment Zones (EZs), the Community Reinvestment Act, and most recently Opportunity Zones all seek to improve low- and moderate-income neighborhoods.[26] But who benefits from these programs, and are the target neighborhoods actually improving?

The first round of federal EZs in the 1990s included sites that were home to 231,438 people in Baltimore, Detroit, and Philadelphia living in neighborhoods with poverty rates from 42 to 50 percent across the three cities (among the original six cities selected for the program). The program offered these neighborhoods a variety of benefits including tax credits to firms that employed people who lived and worked in the zone and block-grant funding that could be used for business assistance, infrastructure development, job training, youth services, and housing services. Research that compared EZ tracts to rejected tracts estimated that the wages of people working in the zones increased overall by $296 million a year, with increases in housing wealth of $1.35 billion.[27] However, other research comparing EZ tracts to non-EZ tracts nearby found negative spillover effects that essentially canceled out the gains of the EZ tracts, demonstrating that what had occurred was simply a spatial reallocation of employment and wages.[28]

Geographically targeted programs such as this often create a type of zero-sum game as economic activity is redistributed from one area to another. In this case, such tax policies do not create new aggregate growth. Instead, they just change where this activity takes place. More can be gained by helping incumbent firms grow and fostering the local quality-of-life conditions that will make firms want to stay.

Investing in Urban Infrastructure

Every city needs good transportation, sewer systems, electricity, school buildings, and water infrastructure. Our cities are old and poor and have a depreciating public-capital stock. This capital stock faces additional challenges from harsh weather, rush-hour traffic, and insufficient maintenance.

While the exact details differ by city, each of these cities must decide whether to defer maintenance or to prioritize capital upgrades. This issue arises for many different government functions. Should schools be renovated? Should water mains be replaced? In each of these cases, questions surround the up-front costs and the long-term benefits achieved by such capital project investments. In Baltimore, aging sewage and water infrastructure has caused sewer backups into many residents' homes.[29] If a city fails to maintain infrastructure, firm productivity and family quality of life will decline, lowering the competitiveness of the city. While this logic encourages cities to invest in infrastructure, the low level of the tax base and concerns about issuing municipal debt make our cities less willing to make these costly investments.

Transit infrastructure is a critical investment in the economic well-being of residents and businesses in cities. A neighborhood lacking access to quality jobs in a short commute will find it difficult to attract residents. However, transportation infrastructure is a costly investment, and cities need to be able to gain financially from their construction. Recent research on the New York City subway showed a 10 percent price increase on real estate near stations, resulting in $7 billion in new property value.[30] In this case, however, the local government did not benefit as much as it could have. Cities need to implement policies that capture the benefits from public investments as much as possible through policies of land value capture.

Given today's low market interest rates, infrastructure projects could be financed by issuing municipal bonds. Institutional investors seek to purchase these bonds to be part of their portfolios. We are surprised that our cities are not being more aggressive in issuing new debt when it is relatively cheap to do so. Macroeconomic work highlights that the interest rate spread (the risk premium that riskier debt must pay relative to risk-free US Treasury bonds) is very low in early 2020.[31] Unfortunately, the COVID-19 crisis will contribute significantly to budget deficits for the federal government and city governments. Baltimore City projected a budget loss of more than $100 million because of COVID-19 and responded by closing vacant positions and realigning government staffing.[32] The net effect of this will be sharp budget cuts. While it is true that infrastructure and "shovel ready" projects are quite attractive to elected officials as a way to create Keynesian stimulus, the realities of the new fiscal situation mean that interest rates could rise for our cities. The willingness of institutional investors to buy local bonds hinges on their perceptions of a city's default risk. Such default risk is lower if the city prospers. This logic again highlights the catch-22 logic that our cities face. By building a reputation for good governance, our cities could do a better job of attracting inflows of capital investment.

Public Safety and Quality of Life

At a time when New York City and Los Angeles have enjoyed a sharp reduction in their murder rates, our six cities continue to have stubbornly high rates. While Baltimore's crime receives frequent media attention, St. Louis and Philadelphia also have a violent crime rate well above the national average.

Business improvement districts (BIDs) and community benefits districts (CBDs) have become popular place-based ways to finance increased safety services in urban neighborhoods. BIDs and CBDs are geographically defined areas where owners of commercial or residential property pay higher taxes for a variety of legislatively defined services, which can include safety, sanitation, workforce development, and other business and residential services. These services are voter approved and are supplemental to baseline city services that businesses and residents receive from the local government.

BIDs demonstrate the synergy between crime reduction and economic development. For example, Philadelphia's Center City District is a BID formed in 1991 by leading businesses in downtown Philadelphia that agreed to implement a commercial property tax to improve the safety and cleanliness of their area, attract new business to locate there, and encourage new customers to visit these businesses. Center City District provides supplemental safety services, homeless outreach, sanitation services, streetscaping, and business services to the district.

BIDs and CBDs provide evidence that homeowners and businesses are willing to pay for an increased level of service to improve their local neighborhood quality of life. These organizations are often more accessible and responsive to local needs than is city government on account of their smaller area. Critics say that BIDs and CBDs do not reduce crime but rather displace it into bordering neighborhoods, widening divides between the haves and the have-nots by improving one neighborhood at the expense of another. Critics also say that only wealthier neighborhoods can afford to pay for these increased services.

We do not know why crime has fallen sharply in cities like Los Angeles and New York City, while it has remained high in other cities.[33] Starting with the early work of Nobel laureate Gary Becker, economists have wrestled with the deterrence question.[34] If a city has demonstrated a high probability of catching criminals and then quickly and severely punishes them, this is severe deterrence. If, however, a city does not clear homicides by arresting suspects, or if the state does not try the case when an arrest is made, then there is no credible threat of punishment, which could increase violence. In Baltimore in early 2020, only 32 percent of violent crimes led to an arrest, with both the mayor of the city and the governor of Maryland continuing to debate how to reduce the city's crime level.

A small number of people commit a large share of urban crimes. If this group could be identified before they commit these crimes, perhaps constructive measures could be taken to both improve their quality of life and discourage them from committing crime. In the science fiction movie *Minority Report*, a police detective played by Tom Cruise uses analytics to anticipate crimes and intercede before they occur. We do not live in that world. But in this age of big data, police departments can construct a database listing the subset of people who have repeatedly been arrested for violent crimes. This subset (mainly young men) are among those most at risk of committing a crime in the future.

Once these individuals have been identified, several possible strategies can discourage crime and build up their human capital. In contrast to severe deterrence, a crime reduction strategy that is gaining popularity focuses on cognitive behavioral therapy tailored to job placement and skill building and to disrupting cycles of poverty. When the Cook County Juvenile Temporary

Detention Center implemented cognitive behavioral therapy, the result was a 21 percent drop in readmissions over 18 months.[35]

A program called Roca, which began in Massachusetts in 1988, expanded to Baltimore in 2018. It seeks to intervene with the most violent criminal offenders by engaging them in positive relationships with credible mentors. The program uses repeated outreach to build deep and transforming relationships and tailors its cognitive and behavioral programming to meet individual needs.

To an economist, the key issue is the program's cost effectiveness. Per dollar spent, how much does it reduce violence? Given that researchers have estimated the social cost of a single homicide at $10 million to $19 million, a small reduction in the number of homicides leads to great economic benefits.[36] For example, it has been estimated that Roca costs $14,000 per trained person per year. If this program reduces the probability of a murder by one percentage point and if the social value of a life is $10 million, then this program is cost effective.

Given scarce budget dollars, such a program competes with other programs. For example, research on the effectiveness of the Safe Streets program in Baltimore has had mixed and at times inconclusive results, with some neighborhoods experiencing significant reductions and others rises in the number of homicides. However, the authors of one study suggest that the program has been under-resourced.[37] It is a politically popular program that has expanded in recent years, which will allow for a more rigorous evaluation.[38]

Recent research has pointed to community investment strategies that might not directly address crime but could result in significant reductions. Research on crime dynamics in Detroit found that vacant buildings, establishments with liquor licenses, and the "right-sizing" of the city's functional footprint were associated with lower levels of violent crime.[39] Vacant lots can become havens for drug dealing and violent criminal activity. A randomized controlled trial in Philadelphia found that vacant lots randomly selected for inexpensive restoration through trash removal and beautification had a 29 percent reduction in gun violence.[40] Sociology research notes the role that nonprofit organizations played in the decline of crime from the 1990s to the 2010s. Each additional set of 10 local nonprofit organizations that focused on reducing violence and building up communities was associated with a 9 percent reduction in the murder rate and a 6 percent reduction in the violent crime rate.[41] These interventions can be complements to the traditional criminal justice system.

A scientific approach to evaluating the independent and synergistic benefits of such crime reduction interventions would be to launch a field experiment. Imagine if Baltimore City could credibly commit to hiring enough detectives to adequately cover the city's homicide caseload. At the same time, the city could quietly choose at random a set of high-crime neighborhoods, and the people living in those neighborhoods deemed to be at high risk of committing future violent crimes would receive interventions through Roca. While a critic would say that this randomization is not fair to the areas that do not receive an expansion of Roca, a poor city such as Baltimore cannot afford to fund a program like Roca citywide with its existing budget commitments. The benefit of rolling out both the deterrence intervention across the city and the behavioral intervention in half the city is that a research team could later evaluate whether violent crime fell by more in the neighborhoods with both the deterrence effect (because detectives had made more arrests) and the behavioral modification treatment.

If the conventional wisdom is that the deterrence effect reduces crime by 10 percent per year and that Roca reduces crime by 5 percent per year, then in the absence of synergy between these programs, we would predict that an area that adopts both of these anti-crime programs would see a 15 percent reduction in crime. If, in fact, this field experiment were launched and crime declined by 30 percent, on average, in the geographic areas that received both the deterrence effect and the Roca program, this result would be evidence of a positive synergy between these two crime prevention programs in achieving their goal. Note that this statistical approach does not explain why this new fact holds true, but it offers a scientific approach because there is an apples-to-apples comparison between the treatment group and the control group, with the control group being those neighborhoods where Roca was not implemented.

Such a field experiment would offer valuable lessons for the other five cities. If an intervention reduces crime in Baltimore, will it have a similar beneficial effect if implemented in Cleveland? Or are there features specific to Baltimore that cannot be "transplanted" to Cleveland? In declaring that a crime prevention program caused a crime reduction, analysts must confront the counterfactual, the economist's what-if. What would a Baltimore neighborhood's crime level have been if the city had not tried the intervention? Given the central role of crime reduction in accelerating economic growth and improving quality of life for our six cities, more experimentation and ex post evaluation are essential.

Significant reductions in homicides in Milwaukee in recent years point to the success that collaboration among law enforcement agencies, researchers, and community partners in data-informed violence reduction strategies can have at the local level.[42] Our cities need to create programs that are both based on evidence and supported by communities if they are to be successful and sustainable.

An economic approach to evaluating these various crime prevention strategies would focus on introducing these policies in a way that is conducive to a rigorous evaluation of the causal effect of each intervention in reducing crime. Such a statistical examination would compare the crime dynamics for a person or a place in the presence of one given policy versus the counterfactual of what the crime dynamics *would have been* without the policy in place. Having made a credible estimate of this effect, an economist would next combine this estimate with the cost of the treatment to calculate the "bang per buck." That is, for each dollar spent on a particular crime reduction intervention, what did society gain? Researchers could then sort comparable findings for multiple interventions from highest to lowest in their value added and thereby identify the most efficient policies. Ideally, this iterative approach to research identifies strategies that are both humane and fair to local residents while also credibly reducing local crime and helping young people achieve their full potential.

Education Policy and School Reform

Skill gaps that open up early will compound over time. A child who is not prepared intellectually or emotionally for kindergarten learns less. Nobel laureate James Heckman has been a leading policy and research champion of early-life skill formation. He has argued that the children of poor people can benefit greatly from increased investment in their skill and early health: "Children from disadvantaged families arrive at kindergarten with a significant achievement gap in the knowledge, vocabulary and social skills necessary to compete and succeed in school. This gap is very difficult to close through remediation, special education and other programs. Quality early childhood education is a vehicle for reducing inequality, not by redistributing wealth, but by *pre-distributing* the wealth of skills and abilities that helps people seize the opportunities of education, healthcare and employment."[43]

Providing prekindergarten education for all three- and four-year-olds would be costly. Maryland has debated how to implement the recommendations of the Kirwan Commission, which called for a variety of investments in education, including an expansion of prekindergarten education. The total cost to implement prekindergarten and other school investments for Baltimore City is estimated to be $330 million a year by 2030, with the State of Maryland spending around $4 billion more.[44]

One of Philadelphia mayor Jim Kenney's signature issues was the soda tax, with revenues directed to funding prekindergarten, schools, parks, recreation centers, and libraries. The soda tax passed, but the effectiveness of the new spending programs is yet unproven, as they have not been in place for long. Oklahoma has had universal prekindergarten at the state level for decades. Research on Tulsa's prekindergarten program has demonstrated large gains in language and cognitive test scores, especially for Hispanic and Black children.[45]

The author of an op-ed in the *Wall Street Journal* has posited that such an expansion would mainly benefit the teachers' union, since teachers' earnings would rise.[46] In a sector that is not governed by competition, an important issue for accountability arises. If more money is earmarked for public schools, who is accountable for ensuring that the money is well spent? One way to ensure this is through regular audits whose results are made publicly available.

In our cities, many public school students are barely graduating and are promoted to the next grade despite low achievement. They are not prepared for the modern workforce. Objective indicators of learning have yielded discouraging results. Recent data from the National Assessment of Educational Progress (NAEP) indicated below-average results for the four of our school districts that participated in the Trial Urban District Assessment (St. Louis and Pittsburgh did not participate). Philadelphia, Baltimore, Cleveland, and Detroit all performed below the national and large-city average in eighth-grade reading and math, with significant percentages of children scoring below NAEP basic levels (figures 6.1 and 6.2). This depressing result is a function of both selection effects and treatment effects. The high level of poverty in our cities sends children to school unprepared, and low resources and school treatment effects mean that the children are not learning at school.

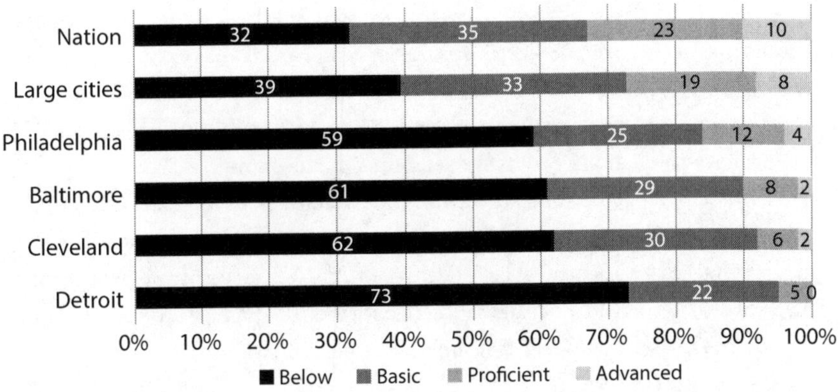

Figure 6.1. Eighth-grade mathematics scores are below average in the four cities that participated in the 2019 National Assessment of Educational Progress.

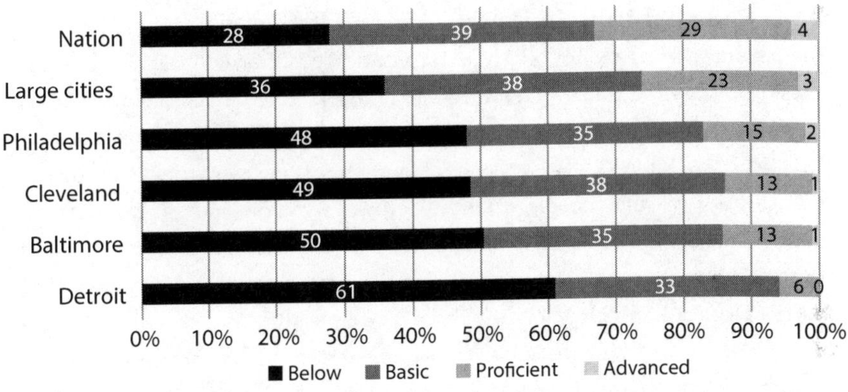

Figure 6.2. Eighth-grade reading scores are below average in the four cities that participated in the 2019 National Assessment of Educational Progress.

In chapter five, we discussed the challenge that young people face in our six cities when they attend public schools segregated by race and income. As economists, we face a fundamental challenge—we do not know the production function for urban education. Consider these possible inputs whose outputs are unknown: If a child from a disadvantaged background has a same-race high-quality teacher, how much of a difference does the teacher make in helping the child escape poverty?[47] If the school has proper air conditioning, how much more does a child learn in May and June?[48] If teachers were paid bonuses for improvements in student test scores, would the schools attract and retain better teachers? And would these teachers invest more effort in acquiring more skill so that they can teach better? How much does the disruption of students who are disciplinary challenges detrimentally impact the learning of other students in the same class?

In discussions of public education, open debates revolve around curricula, student-teacher ratios, and the tracking of students into different classrooms. Many of these debates center on the key issue of the production function for child skill acquisition. If every child has different needs to achieve his or her full potential, how does a public school deliver this tailored education?

Encouraging School Choice

The academic economics community has long debated the role that school choice and competition play in incentivizing innovation. Starting with the work of Milton Friedman, one school of thought has argued that the public sector's monopoly in primary and secondary education discourages innovation. If public schools had to compete to attract students (versus having a geographic catchment area within which all students must attend that school), the leaders and teachers of such schools would have an incentive to improve the schools' quality.[49] However, while competition has offered great benefits in other markets, whether competition would work in this case remains an open question. Critics have argued, for example, that parents lack full information on school quality and so choose schools from a restricted subset of information, owing to barriers such as transportation.

Does competition from Catholic schools and charter schools facilitate public school innovation? Seeing how Uber has disrupted the urban transportation market, could a similar disruption occur in the underperforming public education sector? An evaluation of Maryland's charter school system by Stanford's Center for Research on Education Outcomes found significant benefits for students attending charter schools from 2013 to 2017.[50] Although the research found improved outcomes, especially for minority children, this could be a selection effect from these schools having attracted better students, an issue that requires further investigation.

The economic rationale behind school choice is that increased competition among schools should drive up quality and that parents will be free to choose the school they think best fits the needs of their child. An unintended consequence can be that school choice increases segregation and reduces student achievement.[51] Baltimore City Public Schools has had middle and high school choice since 2005, but this policy has not changed the fact that most schools are segregated by income and race. To investigate the reasons for this fact, researchers interviewed low-income African American students to learn more about the context of choosing a school. They found that students, not their parents, were the ones primarily responsible for deciding where to attend school, and they made their choices in the face of significant barriers, such as limited transportation and the schools their friends attended, which ultimately restricted their selection of a school to a small set that did not maximize educational opportunity.[52]

School choice presents another possible difficulty to students and their parents. When families are free to choose what school to attend, students might opt to attend a school on the other side of the city. This presents an obvious commuting challenge. In Baltimore, many students use the public transit system to get to school, with an average commute time of 36 minutes. Researchers have begun to explore the implications of this commuting on absenteeism.[53]

One promising model that is gaining momentum in the United States is the community school model, which seeks to embed community services in schools (for example, mental health, food pantries, housing stability, adult education, and health center programming). Almost a third of Baltimore's schools are designated community schools. Early evaluations of these schools have shown that they significantly reduce chronic absenteeism and school transfers compared with non-community public schools, providing evidence that they offer students more incentives and support to attend.[54]

While college enrollment rates are low for the students who graduate from our cities' public schools, there is significant variation among high schools, and students face a variety of barriers to college entrance. When students are potentially first-generation college students, and their high schools do not tell them the difference between minimal diploma requirements and university admission requirements, students could think that all colleges and universities are largely the same. Without support from teachers, counselors, and parents, students may not be able to meet the various benchmarks that college entry requires, and they risk entering postsecondary institutions that provide fewer labor market returns after graduation.[55]

We do not claim to know how to deliver high-quality, affordable public education for urban youths. However, given that mobile taxpayers have the option to move to the suburbs, our six cities have a strong incentive to experiment with their delivery of public education.

Housing Policy and Land Use Reform

Every city faces questions of land use policy. In highly desirable cities such as Los Angeles and San Francisco, rules that zone land solely for single-family housing inhibit developers from purchasing adjacent homes and replacing them with multi-family apartment buildings. In New York City, many industrial spaces have been rezoned for residential and commercial use. Google, for example, has purchased stores from Macy's and has reappointed the space to meet its needs. In the new economy, rules need to be flexible enough to allow firms to know what space is available and how a specific location and space can meet their specific needs.

Given our cities' shrinking populations, a major issue for housing and land use revolves around demolishing abandoned and vacant housing. Detroit has made national news for a systematic shrinking of the city. Economic analysis has examined how to create incentives to accelerate redevelopment in areas of the city now restored to green space that have good fundamentals because they are close to the city center.[56] One proposal is a development guarantee such that the government or a third party commits to investing a given amount of money in a specific area of the city that is currently underdeveloped. Such an investment helps to coordinate other interested parties' investments and can create a synergistic effect that helps to renew the area.

Baltimore now has more than 16,000 vacant rowhouses. As the city's population has shrunk from 900,000 to less than 600,000, and as many new housing units have been built in increasingly desirable places such as Harbor East, many homes in the poorest parts of the city have been abandoned. These homes are a magnet for poverty and drug activity. Each of our cities has mapped their abandoned homes and has a plan to demolish or renovate them, but several issues arise. Renovation and demolition are costly and emit lead in the process. Questions surround how the new land will be used once a structure is removed.

Many parcels of land in our cities were zoned for industrial purposes. Now that these industrial activities no longer take place, an opportunity arises for our cities if these parcels can undergo environmental remediation and be repositioned for new uses. Since our cities are situated on waterways, these industrial parcels often have great potential. In the past, their proximity to water reduced transportation costs and provided opportunities for power generation through waterwheels. Now, these parcels have amenity values, since people enjoy living, working, and socializing close to the water. Many of the cities have encouraged waterfront activity through developments such as marinas, restaurants, and parks along the water.[57]

In 2017, Baltimore performed the first comprehensive rewrite of its zoning code in nearly 40 years. In 1971, the last zoning code rewrite prohibited corner stores from new commercial uses. Existing stores were allowed to continue to operate, but as they closed, new businesses were not allowed to open. Given that the structures were built for businesses, they were undesirable as homes and often became vacant. The zoning code rewrite has spurred redevelopment of many of these previously vacant corner properties as commercial properties.

Each of our cities also continues to invest in removing the blight of defunct industrial sites. Ideally, each brownfield (a piece of land that may be contaminated by previous industrial use) can be transformed into a "greenfield." A key issue is the potential of large risks for private investors who worry that they will face liability for future harms suffered on the property.[58] The probability of this scenario is difficult to measure, and this ambiguous risk can scare investors off. This would be especially costly if, for example, a parcel of land with great fundamentals (a beautiful view of the water, say) were not developed because of unfounded liability concerns. If our cities can promise a liability shield, developers would be much more likely to invest in such parcels. For example, the Baltimore Development Corporation makes use of a Brownfields Tax Credit to help businesses overcome impediments to redevelopment of brownfield sites. Since 1996, more than 40 brownfield projects have been completed, which have produced more than 7,000 new or retained jobs and have leveraged more than $500 million in new investment.[59]

One promising housing program discussed earlier in this chapter is Moving to Opportunity, which took place during the late 1990s. The program gave families living in public housing units in several cities, including Baltimore, vouchers to move to private-market rented homes in low-poverty neighborhoods in their city or a surrounding suburb. The impact of this randomized demonstration program has been intensely researched and studied by sociologists, economists, and public health researchers. Raj Chetty and coauthors found that Moving to Opportunity had a profound impact on the outcomes of children who moved to a low-poverty neighborhood before they turned 13 years old. Using tax records, the research team focused on long-term outcomes for children and found that those in Moving to Opportunity (the treatment group) experienced increases in college attendance, earnings, and reductions in single-parenthood rates compared with their control-group peers.[60] Earlier studies found little effect on the employment and earnings outcomes among older youths and adults in the program, as preexisting human-capital barriers, the spatial mismatch of jobs and neighborhoods, and job referral networks acted as strong forces to overcome.[61] Nevertheless, these findings highlight the importance and relatively cheap cost of early childhood intervention programs. Chetty and his research team claim that simply moving to a lower-poverty neighborhood can close almost 25 percent of the gap in lifetime earnings between poor children and their wealthier peers.

Although Moving to Opportunity was a federal program, a similar program called Creating Moves to Opportunity is under way in Seattle. Seattle's program includes a "housing navigator" who helps families receiving vouchers find homes in low-poverty neighborhoods and navigate the ins and outs of negotiating with landlords and adjusting to life in a new neighborhood. One recent study found that families assisted by a housing navigator were much more likely to move to a "high-opportunity" neighborhood.[62] This suggests that there are substantial information barriers to moving to low-poverty areas that offer families better neighborhood satisfaction, and a low-cost intervention of only $2,600 per family could address this issue. As of 2019, 20 other cities around the United States were working on implementing similar programs.[63]

The success of an expanded housing voucher program hinges on several factors. The supply of housing in low-poverty neighborhoods in cities must not be fixed over time. If there is a fixed limit on such housing, then a voucher program will mainly benefit the owners of housing in these neighborhoods, as the subsidy will simply raise rents there. Ideally, a housing voucher subsidy increases the real purchasing power of those who hold a voucher. If they can identify low-poverty neighborhoods and anticipate how they and their children will benefit from living in such neighborhoods, and if the rents do not rise sharply there, then the family can greatly benefit from a voucher program.

One sensitive issue arises. Researchers (including us) who celebrate the apparent success of such voucher programs must recognize that we do not know what would happen if there were a significant expansion of voucher programs. Critics worry that a significant number of poor people moving to a middle-income neighborhood might decrease the neighborhood's quality of life. Residents of Baltimore's suburbs have come out in vocal political opposition to an expansion of Section 8 vouchers because of these fears, stating that it "is a detriment to Baltimore County. Historic neighborhoods, and established communities will see crime, blight, and squalor that is associated with it."[64] While these claims lack evidence, the belief that this effect will occur generates political opposition. Anticipating this effect, those who design a voucher expansion program could build in safeguards so that voucher recipients do not concentrate in a few areas but instead spread out across many middle-class neighborhoods. This should attenuate concerns about significant negative effects for neighborhoods.

Benchmarking the Quality of Governance

Devising an apples-to-apples comparison of governance quality across cities is surprisingly difficult. Earlier in this chapter, we provided brief biographies of the mayors of each of the six cities. We do not know how to rank them with report cards for who is doing the best job. Which one has been most effective at reducing crime, accelerating economic growth, and improving public services? If we as academics cannot judge this, how can the electorate?

We also do not have compelling tests of the role of urban leadership. For example, if Michael Bloomberg were the mayor of Baltimore, would the murder rate quickly decline by 50 percent? At any point in time, cross-city variation in crime and school quality is a function of local policies, yet it is also a function of many other variables over which the mayor has little control. Because of this trouble in benchmarking local leaders, they have some "wiggle room" to make the case that they are succeeding.

Incentives for Urban Policy Experimentation

Given their cold winters and relatively low levels of human capital, our six cities have to offer great governance per tax dollar to compete with rival cities and suburbs for footloose firms and people. Each of these cities is grappling with how to improve the quality of basic public services, ranging from street safety to schooling to transportation to workforce skill development. Economists advocate for field experiments when they do not know the answer to a question. The 2019 Nobel Prize in Economics was awarded to three scholars who demonstrated the power of running and learning from field experiments in the developing world. The leaders of our cities would be wise to embrace this perspective. While there is some degree of experimentation in the cities, more is needed to identify those policies that work and those that do not.

The methodology of a field experiment uses randomization to determine a subject's status in either the treatment or control group. This random assignment guarantees that those in the treatment group and those in the control group are, on average, similar at baseline. Such randomization raises the likelihood that any ex post differences between the average treatment subject and the average control are actually an effect of the treatment.

Unfortunately, many mayors are reluctant to follow this methodology. Ideally, a group of mayors would form a learning consortium and agree to run the same experiment in each of their cities. This would foster a type of urban laboratory, with the resulting impacts being quantified and compared across the cities. Given the demand for safe streets, vocational training, good childcare, and clean streets, the puzzle is why these cities are not experimenting more to better supply these needed services.

The reluctance to engage in more experimentation suggests that urban government inefficiency will persist. In 1966, Harvey Leibenstein introduced the idea of "X-inefficiency" in economics, which has crucial implications for explaining persistent inefficiency in providing key public services in our cities.[65] X-inefficiency arises because of weak incentives. For example, a police department that pays police a fixed salary may do little policing in dangerous neighborhoods because such neighborhoods pose risks for the police. In this setting, taxpayers will pay the salaries for these employees, but crime will not decline. These inefficiencies could decline if each community knew who its police officers were and could report to city authorities if crime was rising and the police were not investigating. Such accountability would reduce X-inefficiency.

In any government organization, whether it is the police or the teachers, there is a question of how the city builds a quality workforce. Does it pay high salaries and offer good benefits to attract great people who have strong outside alternatives? Or does it broadly hire and then offer great skills development and weed out those who are ineffective? Does the organization have a culture that makes people feel valued and celebrates individual excellence? What are the social and economic incentives within the organization for encouraging effort and keeping up morale?

Baltimore City has shown some promise in attracting young, skilled staff. In 1999, Baltimore mayor Martin O'Malley began implementing CitiStat, which is based on the New York City Police Department's CompStat. The program required computer-savvy staff doing data analysis to evaluate the service delivery efforts of various agencies. For example, the program reduced the time it took the city to remove an abandoned vehicle by around 60 percent. With an annual budget of $400,000, the program saved an estimated $12 million in its first year.[66] In 2019, the city opened the Mayor's Office of Performance and Innovation, staffed mostly by young designers and data analysts who look to solve various issues that the city faces. In contrast, a recent audit of the Baltimore Police Department found a lack of technology and reliance on paper-intensive manual systems, including scheduling and timekeeping, which resulted in a "lack of controls to limit overtime waste, fraud and abuse."[67]

Local government agencies have considerable private information about their day-to-day activities, but it is very difficult for outsiders to monitor their activities. This "asymmetric information" gives urban public employees room to pursue their own agenda. Given that many of them have secure employment and do not have the opportunity to earn bonus pay, they do not have strong incentives to devote extra effort to their jobs. In such a setting, bureaucratic inertia can persist because nobody in the organization has an incentive to try new experimental things that may pose a threat to an incumbent interest group. The public sector in this setting is a monopolist and does not have to fear the kind of disruption that entities such as Uber have posed for the taxi industry. In this sense, urban government exemplifies the "quiet life of the monopolist."[68]

In theory, voters could hold government officials accountable on election day, but they face the challenge of figuring out the extent of the X-inefficiency. How could voters have sufficient imagination and information to foresee how much better the local schools and street safety would be if an experimenter served as the city's mayor?

In making these points, we do not seek to challenge the character of the people who work in city government. Instead, we want to highlight the social costs of the current game in which participants face too little competition. In a competitive environment where effort is costly, workers will be more likely to bear these costs if they see a chance of being promoted to a more desirable job. Without the discipline of market competition, city government agencies have weak incentives to adopt best practices. Because of the relatively low pay and few opportunities for rising in the organization, the skilled and ambitious are less likely to want these jobs.

Would public-sector productivity be higher if some functions were privatized? In Latin America, for example, many bus routes have been privatized.[69] However, the privatization of water utilities has proved unpopular and ineffective in Uruguay, which banned water privatization in 2004, and in Berlin, which ended a contract with Veolia and bought back shares in the face of public opposition. Research by Werner Troesken has highlighted that private water companies often lack the financial incentive to provide clean and safe water for poor and minority residents.[70] In 2018, Baltimore became the first large US city to ban water privatization in the wake of the lead crises in Flint and Pittsburgh and concerns that the city would not be able to control rate increases.

This ongoing contentious debate over privatization of some government services highlights the importance of relying on experts to carefully consider the issues on a case-by-case basis. Experts can disclose their assumptions and explain their modeling techniques while providing a clear ex ante perspective on how much the winners stand to win and the losers are likely to lose from a major change in how urban services are delivered. Given the fundamental uncertainty in such an analysis, a wise policy approach would build in "option value" to allow for future changes in agreements and rules that can be introduced as the city learns about the consequences of privatization.

A possible middle ground between the public and private sectors are quasi-government organizations. These are government-controlled nonprofit organizations that are privately run and have aspects of both public and private organizations. They can take different forms and serve a variety of purposes, but essentially they enable governments to do things they otherwise would not be able to do. A well-known example is the City and Port Development Corporation of Copenhagen, Denmark. In the 1980s, national and local officials came together to form the corporation with the goal of catalyzing the development of underutilized city assets for public gain. The entity oversaw the redevelopment of a city harbor that ultimately financed an expanded public transit system. Our cities should consider the benefits that combining the efficiency of the private sector with the accountability and direction of the public sector could bring to redevelopment goals.[71]

If Michael Bloomberg had been elected mayor of one of our cities, he might have used his clout to run experiments. In the private sector, he has focused on how to acquire market share in a competitive environment where a product consistently faces the market test of whether anyone will buy it. He made billions from processing and delivering information, competing against other information providers and designing Bloomberg terminals (a computer software system for accessing proprietary Bloomberg LP financial data) to meet the needs of those who demanded this product.

Our cities are managed mostly by career politicians. At the risk of overgeneralizing, such insiders lack experience with different ways of delivering service. The inherent modesty of field experimenters requires constant humility, since they do not know how best to deliver quality public education, safe streets, efficient garbage pickup, and public transit. While to some this may sound like admitting weakness, we view it as signaling strength. In our big data age, cities now have the ability to collect and disseminate data about real-time activity taking place across the city. Data-informed metrics of performance combined with field experiments offer an iterative approach to learning what works.

NOTES

1. Bertrand and Mullainathan 2001.
2. Jerch, Kahn, and Li 2017; DiSalvo 2015.
3. Anderson 2020.
4. Feuer 2013.
5. Cornish 2014.
6. Kreiss and McGregor 2018.
7. Maskin 2018.
8. Alesina and Glaeser 2004.
9. Dennis and Selway 2020.
10. Katz and Nowak 2017.
11. Open Baltimore, BPD employee file.
12. Rutkow, McGinty, Wetter, and Vernick 2019.
13. DuPuis, Langan, McFarland, Panettieri, and Rainwater 2018.
14. Warnock 2015.
15. Glaeser 2020.
16. Kleine 2019.
17. Baltimore City Bureau of the Budget and Management Research.
18. Fire and Police Employee's Retirement System of the City of Baltimore 2019.

19. Branas, Suoth, Kondo, Hohl, Bourgois, Wiebe, and MacDonald 2018.
20. Wilen 2018; Renn 2019.
21. Bergman, Chetty, DeLuca, Hendren, Katz, and Palmer 2019; Chetty, Hendren, and Katz 2016.
22. Joassart-Marcelli, Musso, and Wolch 2005.
23. Gyourko and Summers 1997.
24. Slattery and Zidar 2020.
25. Bartik 2019.
26. Neumark and Koko 2010.
27. Busso, Gregory, and Kline 2013.
28. Hanson and Rohlin 2013.
29. Richman 2019, "Not acceptable."
30. Gupta, Nieuwerburgh, and Kontokosta 2020.
31. Breckenridge Capital Advisors 2020.
32. Opilo 2020.
33. Levitt 2004.
34. Becker 1968; Kleiman 2009.
35. Ideas42 2017.
36. Abt 2019.
37. Webster, Buggs, and Crifasi 2018.
38. Rodricks 2020.
39. Raleigh and Galster 2015.
40. Branas, South, Kondo, Hohl, Bourgois, Wiebe, and MacDonald. 2018.
41. Sharkey, Torrats-Espinosa, and Takyar 2017.
42. Watson 2020.
43. Heckman Equation 2014.
44. Richman 2019, Baltimore mayor.
45. Gormley, Phillips, and Anderson 2018.
46. Riley 2019.
47. Gershenson, Hart, Hyman, Lindsay, and Papageorge 2019.
48. Park, Goodman, Hurwitz, and Smith 2020.
49. Hoxby 2000.
50. Charter School Performance in Maryland 2019.
51. Abdulkadiroğlu, Pathak, and Walters 2018; Willms 2000.
52. Condliffe, Boyd, and DeLuca 2015.
53. Stein, Grigg, Cronister, Chavis, and Connolly 2017.
54. Durham and Connolly 2016.
55. Durham, Stein, and Connolly 2015.
56. Owens, Rossi-Hansberg, and Sarte 2020.
57. Kramer 2019.
58. Sigman 1998, 2010; Chang and Sigman 2000.
59. Baltimore Development Corporation.
60. Chetty, Hendren, and Katz 2016.
61. Turney, Clampet-Lundquist, Edin, Kling, and Duncan 2006.
62. Bergman, Chetty, DeLuca, Hendren, Katz, and Palmer 2019.
63. Kristof 2019.
64. Zumer 2019.
65. Leibenstein 1966.
66. Government Innovators Network.
67. Baltimore City Department of Finance 2018.
68. Alchian and Kessel 1962.
69. Gomez-Ibanez and Meyer 2011.
70. Troesken 2004.
71. Katz and Noring 2017.

7

Promising Trends

Around the world, young and old people increasingly desire urban living. This trend creates a new opportunity for our cities to be rediscovered as affordable places to both live and visit. Global reductions in the costs of transportation and information enhance this opportunity. Cheaper and more frequent air travel is allowing more people to visit cities. Platforms such as Airbnb and Couchsurfing give people more ways to experience a city without visiting tourist traps. Our six cities tend to be ranked high as "underrated" cities that appeal to travelers looking for more original experiences and to millennials looking for fun and relatively cheap places to start their careers.[1]

Both demand-side factors and supply-side factors offer an optimistic outlook on the potential for progress.

The Rising Demand for a Consumer City

Urban living is in high demand. Cell phone technology and the app economy have placed a premium on living downtown. In the past, when we did not have our own cell phones and internet access, high search costs limited our ability to find friends, restaurants, and things to do in cities. Today, using electronic devices that connect to the internet, urbanites coordinate their activity in cities and use ride sharing to get around town. They use Yelp and other services to avoid being fooled into patronizing tourist traps. Easy access to reservations allows people to save time by not waiting in line. The net result is a greater gain from the urban lifestyle.[2] This effect is further accentuated in cities with low pollution and street safety.[3]

All six of the cities have strong consumer city fundamentals, with good restaurants, art districts, museums, live theater, major sports teams, neighborhoods with beautiful architecture, parks and waterfronts, and cultural amenities. They are all close to water and offer the possibility of synergies between urban living and water, as Boston, New York City, and San Francisco have demonstrated. Recognizing this, many of our cities have begun to redevelop their waterfronts and market them to tourists and residents alike.

Our cities all have flourishing arts, entertainment, and dining scenes. In 2017, Zagat rated Baltimore, Detroit, St. Louis, and Philadelphia among its top 30 most exciting food cities in America. New varieties of restaurants continue to open. Our six cities are home to more than 450 museums and feature countless cultural attractions, including the Detroit Institute of Arts, the Philadelphia Museum of Art, the Barnes Foundation, the Rock and Roll Hall of Fame, the Cleveland Museum of Art, City Museum, the St. Louis Arch, and the National Aquarium.[4] Many of these institutions attract more than half a million local, regional, and international visitors annually. Many of the best venues for dining and entertainment are still located in center cities, including restaurants, concert halls, art galleries, playhouses, and sports stadiums. While wealthy people who work in the city may retreat to the suburbs after work, they spend a significant amount of their leisure time in cities attending cultural events and dining.

Cities that can offer a high-quality urban consumer experience will enjoy economic growth because wealthy people will patronize their businesses. Urban downtowns are job hubs, but they empty out at night as people working at those high-paying jobs go home to the suburbs. Baltimore's downtown and Seton Hill neighborhood was home to 6,533 people in 2017, but 78,158 worked there during the day, and many of these people do not live in neighborhoods close to downtown. For decades, richer people were drawn to the suburbs because of newer and more spacious housing, private space, fear of crime, and weak urban public schools. Facing this reality, city boosters face the marketing challenge of how to convince people to live in the city.[5]

Urban economists have argued that cities must feature enough activity for specialized stores to sell to customers profitably.[6] On weekends, people spend more time shopping and enjoying leisure outside when they are in a safe, attractive environment, and suburbanites will be more willing to visit the city to experience the culture and the variety of products and experiences that they cannot find in their lower-density suburbs.

While Philadelphia and Pittsburgh have enjoyed more success in recent years in terms of population and job growth, all our cities have witnessed reductions in the population of poor families and increases in the share of wealthy families. Median income grew in all the cities from 2010 to 2018, with the largest increase in Pittsburgh (a $10,422 increase in Allegheny County) and the smallest increase in Detroit (a $3,080 increase in Wayne County). The share of families with incomes of less than $50,000 a year decreased in all our cities, while the share of families with incomes of more than $100,000 a year grew in all. For example, St. Louis had 4,211 fewer families with incomes of less than $10,000 in 2018 than in 2010 and 2,950 more families with incomes over $200,000. All our cities have benefited from booms in the national economy.

Given lingering safety concerns, this rise of the consumer city will benefit those parts of the city that are perceived to be safest. If the six cities make strong progress in reducing violent crime, more parts of the city will become part of the nascent consumer city. More parts of the city will thrive as people go out more at night and explore. Such serendipitous exploration of the city will build trust and mutual understanding as people visit parts of the city that in the past they would not have dared to visit.

The Rising Demand for a Green City

Richer, more educated young people seek to live and work and play in "green cities." Many young progressives want to live in a city that "walks the walk" in terms of not exacerbating the threat of climate change. Each of our six cities is already offering a green urbanite lifestyle that people increasingly demand.

A city's environmental performance is determined both by global criteria, such as its carbon footprint per capita and climate resilience, and by local criteria, such as whether it offers clean air, clean water, and green space. Recent literature in environmental economics has stressed the key role that low-pollution environments play in developing human capital.[7] Put simply, both children at school and workers at their jobs have more trouble thinking in more polluted settings. Thus, as our cities reduce pollution, more human capital can be developed, and this human capital can be better used.

In the past, high levels of industrial and transportation activity along the water in these cities caused much pollution and localized disamenities. By 2020, a silver lining of deindustrialization has been that these past manufacturing hubs have transitioned, and many, such as Fells Point in Baltimore, have embraced their niche as a high-amenity urban neighborhood. With their adjacency to water, our cities offer great opportunities for walking and exercise in settings of great beauty. If our six cities can offer such opportunities, more people will consider living there.

At a time of great concern about climate change, some of these cities are making efforts to reduce their carbon footprint. For economists, the free rider problem is important. In a world of almost eight billion people, the total greenhouse gas emissions from our six cities, which are home to 3.5 million people, is tiny. Given this logic, the key climate change issue for these cities is their resilience. As summers become hotter and as the sea level rises, how will these cities plan for the emerging but ambiguous new threats we face? If our cities gain a reputation for being eco-friendly, they will attract young residents who are passionate about environmental issues.

Baltimore's recent banning of single-use plastic bags and polystyrene food containers is an example of this trend. Businesses located around Baltimore's Inner Harbor have helped fund an effort to prevent trash from flowing into the ocean by paying for several trash wheels. The city also has a concerted effort in partnership with nonprofits and residents to increase the tree canopy to reduce the urban heat island effect and improve health outcomes. Throughout this book, we have emphasized the importance of competition among cities for people and jobs. A city that earns a reputation for being green, in its physical beauty and its environmental policies, is likely to be in higher demand among young, educated people.

Just as there is a synergy between reducing street crime and local real estate investment, a more pleasant ambiance close to the water creates incentives for stores and investors to upgrade local areas. Those who seek variety in the form of organic food markets and distinctive entertainment will gain more from such experiences if the outdoor environmental conditions are pleasant.

Environmental Progress

Each of our six cities has made significant progress in reducing pollution levels and some environmental health risks. While nationally there has been around a 30 percent reduction in PM2.5 (small particulate matter, the main measure of air pollution) from 2000 to 2018, our cities have experienced even more significant reductions of around 50 percent.

Although each of our cities benefited from being a manufacturing hub, manufacturing is highly polluting. As these cities have transitioned away from heavy manufacturing, the combination of cleaner air and cleaner water has offered both aesthetic pleasures and health benefits.

Each of our cities has experienced significant declines in recent decades in the number of children exposed to lead (figure 7.1).[8] In the early 1990s in Baltimore, over 30 percent of children tested had elevated blood lead levels, defined as over 10 micrograms per deciliter. This rate now stands at 1 percent in Baltimore. However, there is no safe level of lead exposure, and in 2012 the Centers for Disease Control and Prevention defined a lead level of 5 micrograms per deciliter as elevated. By this measure, a significant number of children are still being poisoned, and our cities are still dealing with the legacy of high lead exposure rates from the 1990s and early 2000s.

An association between early-life lead exposure and later violent criminal activity may bear on this problem.[9] Early lead exposure is associated with a lower IQ and an increased risk of attention deficit disorder. These outcomes are associated with a higher propensity to commit violent crimes because affected individuals have self-control problems. In our recent research using data from neighborhoods in Baltimore, Buffalo, Chicago, and Detroit, we documented that African Americans are exposed to more lead

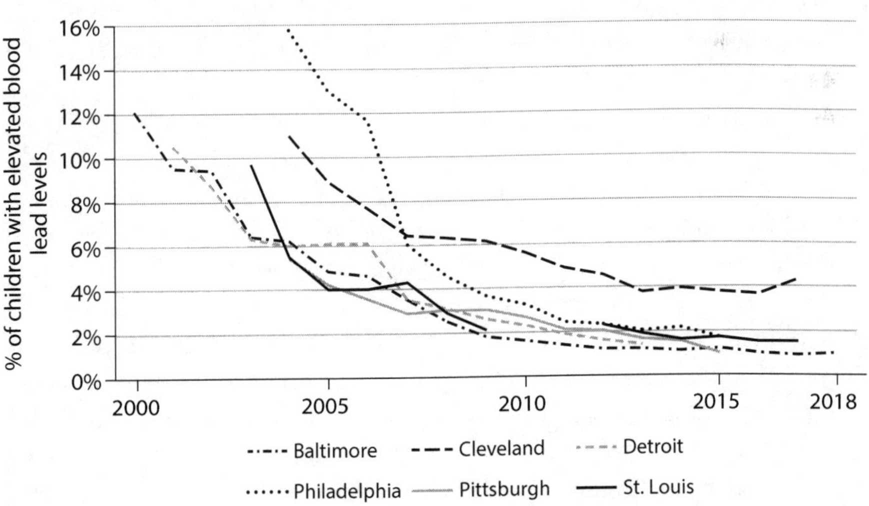

Figure 7.1. The number of children with elevated levels of lead in their blood fell from the early part of the 21st century through 2018.

than other groups because Black children are more likely to grow up in older housing in center cities or in neighborhoods closer to old industrial sites and highways. The good news is that lead exposure rates are declining. This means that the correlation between race and violence is likely to shrink.

In recent years, cities have continued to make major investments in reducing water pollution by investing in waste treatment plants.[10] Much of this investment has been mandatory through Environmental Protection Agency (EPA) consent decrees following violations of the Clean Water Act. These are multibillion-dollar investments in stormwater and sewer infrastructure aimed at reducing combined-sewer runoff into local waterways.

In 2012, the EPA approved Philadelphia's Green City, Clean Waters initiative to increase green stormwater infrastructure over 25 years at a cost of $2 billion.[11] This plan aims to reduce the amount of stormwater before it reaches the city's pipes and so decrease the chance of overflows. In contrast, Baltimore's EPA consent decree focuses on upgrades to the Back River Wastewater Treatment Plant and sewage main repairs, which represent investments in gray rather than green infrastructure. These repairs are crucial for the quality of life of local residents, as sewage can back up into homes and cause thousands of dollars of repairs. However, critics of the plan fear that it will do nothing to improve the health of the harbor and local waterways.[12] In addition, there is a clear demand for clean waterways as local companies have funded waterway cleanup efforts in Baltimore's Inner Harbor through the Waterfront Partnership, recognizing the importance of the harbor as a place for leisure activity.

In addition to air and water pollution, cities are increasingly aware of the new climate risks they face from rising temperatures and sea levels. Cities that are better prepared to meet these risks will have a greater supply of safe neighborhoods and will suffer less from the emerging threat. Recognizing the risks, our research center at John Hopkins University, the 21st Century Cities Initiative, has partnered with the First Street Foundation to help Baltimore City plan for the challenge of a rising sea level. In this project, we will provide Baltimore City with state-of-the-art flood risk maps to help the city foresee new threats to land and to residential and commercial properties. This forewarning will allow the city to consider its land use policies and to think through where economic development should be nudged to build a more resilient city with a greater potential to thrive over the next few decades.

Immigrant Demand for Local Housing

Each year, more international immigrants are moving to our cities. While the populations of our cities are declining, with the exception of Pittsburgh, this reduction would be even larger in the absence of international immigration (figure 7.2). If not for international immigrants, our cities would have lost an additional 180,000 people from 2010 to 2018. In 2017, over half of these immigrants came from Asia, with a further 17 percent from Europe and 11 percent from Africa.

Attracting immigrants has been a particular strength of Baltimore, Detroit, Philadelphia, and St. Louis over the past two decades, with Cleveland and Pittsburgh lagging somewhat behind. From 2000 to 2017, all our cities witnessed growth in the share and total number of the foreign-born population.[13] In 2000, our cities' share of foreign-born population ranged from 3.8 percent in Pittsburgh (Allegheny County) to 9 percent in Philadelphia. By 2017, this share had risen to 5.7 percent in Pittsburgh and 13.8 percent in Philadelphia. Baltimore witnessed the fastest growth in immigrant population, with an increase of 67 percent over the period, from nearly 30,000 to nearly 50,000. By comparison, the foreign-born population of the United

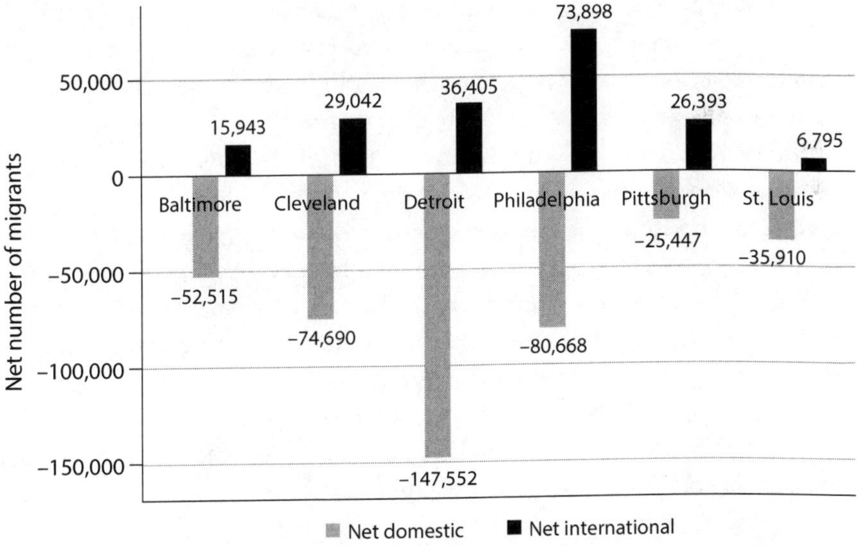

Figure 7.2. Positive net international migration partly compensated for negative net domestic migration in the six cities from 2010 through 2018. Source: American Community Survey, 5 Year

States was 11 percent in 2000 and 13 percent in 2017. So while our cities started behind the national average in 2000, several of them are quickly catching up.

Economists point out that immigrants represent a select sample of their origin nation's population.[14] They are the subset of people with the desire and the grit to leave their home country. They tend to be better educated and wealthier, giving them the financial capacity to bear the migration costs to move to an unfamiliar place. Such individuals are likely to contribute to their destination by either starting new businesses or providing skills that are in demand. This logic suggests that if our cities compete for immigrants, aggregate housing demand will increase, local home prices will stabilize or rise, and renovation and upgrading of the capital stock will be more likely. In this case, more tax revenue will be available to use for improving public goods.[15]

St. Louis is well known for its German immigrants, including Adolphus Busch, who went on to found the successful Anheuser-Busch brewery. A more recent wave of immigrants came to the city in the midst of the Bosnian War in the 1990s, clustering in particular neighborhoods such as Bevo. There are more Bosnians per capita in St. Louis than anywhere in the world outside Bosnia. Given that immigrants often want to bring with them a taste of home and maintain a connection to their homeland, they tend to open restaurants, bars, and other cultural establishments that often become popular beyond the immediate immigrant community.

But how did the St. Louis metro area suddenly become home to 70,000 Bosnians? In this case, it largely came down to the US State Department's coordination with local agencies to determine housing availability, the number of entry-level job openings, and the ability of a community to incorporate a large number of new immigrants.[16] There is another factor at work, though, in concentrating immigrant communities: chain migration and secondary migration. If someone immigrates, say, from Burundi to Detroit, finds success, and tells family, friends, and relatives back home of this success, then those who hear the good news are much more likely to immigrate to Detroit than someplace else and will inform their broader network in turn, thus spurring others to make the same journey. These reliable messengers provide trustworthy information that one could not glean from a Google search. This is exactly what has happened in Detroit, with a growing number of immigrants from countries like Burundi and Bangladesh starting successful businesses with the help of local economic development agencies such as Global Detroit, Motor City Match, and Hatch Detroit.[17]

Each of the six cities is home to one or more major university that attracts both domestic and international students, faculty, and staff. Since these universities are committed to remaining in our six cities, their future reputation matters to the economic vitality of their locations. University leaders recognize that they are important stakeholders in improving their cities. Johns Hopkins University's president Ron Daniels has emphasized that it is in the university's enlightened self-interest to invest "in the role that our faculty, students, and staff play in our public school system, in the many contributions that our schools and health systems have made to address the pressing health needs of our city, [and] in the energy and financial resources we have invested in the very ambitious and worthy project that is aimed at restoring our city's east side as a safe, prosperous, and vibrant community."[18] Universities such as the University of Pennsylvania and Hopkins solve a coordination problem as promising young scholars move to learn and work at these campuses. This also attracts start-up companies to locate nearby. Our cities seem to be particularly adept at recognizing and acting on this opportunity. For example, Baltimore created the Mayor's Office of Immigrant and Multicultural Affairs in 2013 as part of a broader goal of attracting and retaining immigrants to grow the city's population.

Of particular concern to our cities are recent changes in US foreign policy. After leading the world for decades in the number of refugee resettlements, ranging from 70,000 a year to 207,000 a year from 1980 to 2000, the United States set the refugee cap at 18,000 for fiscal year 2020, the lowest number since the 1980 Refugee Act passed.[19] All US cities that have reversed population loss since the 1980s have had significant growth in international migrants.[20] If our cities continue to lose out on net domestic migration, they will be increasingly unable to offset this loss with the arrival of international migrants.

Real Estate Conversion and New Housing Supply

Today, one of us (Kahn) lives in a brand-new building on the site of a defunct chromium plant that went out of business 30 years ago. The apartment offers a great view of the water and has easy access to nearby restaurants and upscale stores.[21] In this new building in Baltimore, rent is more than $3 per square foot per month.

The *Baltimore Sun* has explained the property's transition from low-amenity industrial site to its shiny new Harbor East present.[22] In 1989, the owner of the property, Allied-Signal, Inc., signed a consent decree that required the company to remove all of its buildings and cover the site to protect people from toxic dust. Allied armored the shoreline against erosion and installed a barrier of clay and clean soil down to bedrock around the site perimeter to keep tainted groundwater from reaching the Patapsco River. Honeywell, which inherited Allied's assets and environmental liabilities, has continued to pump and treat groundwater to keep it from getting into the river and has maintained monitoring of the site.

In Baltimore, real estate developers are making big bets that wealthy people want to live downtown by building tall apartment towers such as 414 Light Street and 1301 Aliceanna Sreet. In the nearby historic neighborhood of Fells Point, developers have been converting old commercial space, factories, and warehouses into mixed-used redevelopment, often using New Markets Tax Credits from the federal government. Closer to Johns Hopkins's main Homewood campus, significant redevelopment in Remington has focused on small-scale rowhouse development and mixed-use buildings.

The redevelopment of the Remington neighborhood is an interesting case study in how a developer can focus on the revitalization of a single neighborhood. Around 2007, working with a group of teachers who wanted discounted apartments in Baltimore, Seawall Development began doing work in Remington. The company did not choose the neighborhood but instead found a property there that it could redevelop. Seawall had originally seen this as a one-off development, but through this project the company established close ties with the community. Other teachers signaled that they would purchase redeveloped rowhouses if Seawall renovated them, so the company expanded its work. The community noticed and began to work with the developer to redevelop vacant properties.

In discussions with community members, Seawall learned that the neighborhood lacked commercial assets such as a bank, dry cleaners, restaurants, doctor's offices, and barbershops. Legacy residents were particularly excited, as they remembered the good old days of Remington and wanted to see the neighborhood return to prosperity. Since their first set of affordable houses for teachers, Seawall has done a number of mixed-use developments, including Remington Row, R. House, and FastForward.

However, the developer did not realize how popular these new investments would be, and an unanticipated consequence was a sharp rise in neighborhood rents. Community members have tried to address this problem by starting Remington Community Land Trust to create and maintain permanently affordable housing that is community owned. Seawall's advice to other developers in urban areas is to listen closely to the people in the communities they are working in and not to go in with any preconceived notions of what is best.

Drug Legalization

As of 2020, medical marijuana was legal in the states of Maryland, Michigan, Missouri, Ohio, and Pennsylvania and is, therefore, legal in all six of our cities. While marijuana is not fully legalized in any of these states, all appear to be making progress toward full legalization. In their first year of legalization, these states had sales ranging from $58.3 million in Ohio to $132 million in Pennsylvania. The State of Michigan expected to generate $18 million in tax revenue in its first year of taxing medical marijuana. If these states were to legalize marijuana completely, they could expect to bring in even more revenue that could be used to fund anti-poverty programs and to ameliorate some of the worst damage done to these cities by the War on Drugs. But how could this money be spent? We will look at the State of Colorado as an example.

From February 2014, when the state legalized marijuana, through January 2020, Colorado generated total revenue of $1.2 billion from taxes, licenses, and fees. In Colorado, the majority of state funding goes to school construction and operating costs.[23] While $300 million in annual revenue from taxing marijuana sales might seem like a lot, it accounts for less than 1 percent of the total state budget. Similarly, the revenues from marijuana taxes in Maryland of between $50 million and $200 million per year represent a small part of the state's $46 billion annual budget.[24] State and local governments should not look to the legalization of marijuana as a panacea for funding ambitious new programs and interventions. Yet, when coupled with a reduction in spending on public safety and criminal justice through fewer low-level drug arrests, these funds could have a significant impact on state and local government finances.

Drug legalization creates a potentially exciting natural experiment. Could urban street violence decline sharply after drug legalization? Imagine a case where young men fight for turf, the street corners, in order to have an edge in selling drugs. If drugs can be legally sold at convenience stores, these private spaces will replace public spaces as the marketplace. Economists discuss the tragedy of the commons, which contends that public property is not treated as well as private property after public resources are privatized. Drug dealer violence exemplifies this point.[25]

Reductions in drug-dealing violence and the short-run economic opportunities afforded by drug dealing would have a beneficial impact on young men's educational attainment. Recognizing that they cannot turn a profit in drug dealing, these young men might invest more in their schooling, thereby increasing their economic potential in the legal labor market.[26]

However, while states are increasingly legalizing marijuana, many other drugs are still sold illegally, including heroin, methamphetamine, opioids, and cocaine, and these are very unlikely to be legalized by any state. Selling them will remain a profitable illegal business for drug dealers, including people living in poverty in our cities, so drug dealing will likely never vanish entirely from our cities.

One concern that has been raised in Maryland is that the barriers to entry in opening a dispensary or growing marijuana are too high. As a result, the same population that was punished and jailed when marijuana was completely illegal during the War on Drugs is now being kept out of the legal marketplace. A 2017 study of these concerns paid for by the State of Maryland found significant adverse disparities for minority- and women-owned businesses in wages, salaries, business owner earnings, and business formation rates in the marijuana industry.[27] If entrepreneurs are effectively denied entry because of high barriers, minority business owners stand to lose from the profits generated by this industry.

Smart Cities and the Rise of Urban Information Technology

Back in the 1990s, when a dead animal or debris was found on the city streets, somebody would have to call the city government, someone on the staff would have to answer the call and make a note in paper records, and a team would need to go out and address the issue. Flash-forward to the year 2020, and every city has a 311 app allowing citizens to report municipal issues in an electronic database. Cities can then post these reported cases to the internet on an open data portal and include information about when the city addressed the issue. This dynamic accountability empowers residents to engage with city government.

The data creation process creates benchmarks for citizens to judge how their city is performing. A critic, however, could argue that standardized experiments are not taking place. Imagine a field experiment where piles of garbage are left at random locations within our six cities. A test of effective government could be to measure how long it takes for somebody to report the garbage and then for the garbage to be cleaned up. When the garbage is dumped in a poor part of Cleveland, does the government respond more slowly than it does when the garbage appears in a rich part of Cleveland?

The rise of urban big data promotes citizen democracy through accountability. Such data allow researchers and the media to benchmark cities over time. For example, posting the pay of public employees allows researchers to compare overtime pay across cities to see which ones have the most police officers earning more than $150,000 a year. Letting in the sunshine when it comes to city administration promotes an honest dialogue because urban leaders are aware that outliers will make the news. This encourages such organizations to engage in self-regulation.

Synergies

Throughout this chapter, we have discussed several promising demand-side and supply-side trends that boost our optimism about the possibility of a strong comeback for our six cities. These various "puzzle pieces" are interconnected and offer exciting synergistic possibilities.

For example, if a real estate developer is confident that policing will reduce crime in an area, the developer may upgrade a structure and make the area nicer. However, a coordination failure could occur instead if the developer does not make the upgrade because the developer expects the area to continue to be dangerous or if the police do not prioritize the area because it features crumbling buildings.

Avoiding coordination failures in which private-sector investors and the government both underinvest in an area requires confidence, good luck, and, most important of all, communication so that the parties involved can learn to work together and trust each other. A basic idea from game theory is the notion of a repeated game. If investors and government officials have worked together successfully in the past, this builds trust and mutual understanding and encourages each party to invest. Such self-interest helps to build stronger cities on the basis of mutual interests. In recent history, many neighborhoods in these cities have suffered from coordination failures that led to too little investment by people, government, and firms. We believe, however, that the promising forces discussed in this chapter can set in motion a series of new investments, which together can help these cities and their residents unlock the benefits of economic growth.

NOTES

1. Kiersz 2013; Amsden 2017; Olander 2019.
2. Handbury and Weinstein 2014.
3. Gaspar and Glaeser 1998.
4. Institute of Museum and Library Services 2018.
5. Monroe 2019; Zurawik 2018.
6. Waldfogel 2008.
7. Graff, Zivin, and Neidell 2013.
8. Maryland Department of the Environment 2019; Pennsylvania Department of Health; Cuyahoga County Board of Health; Michigan Department of Health and Human Services; City of St. Louis, Department of Health 2018.
9. Manduca and Sampson 2019.
10. Jerch 2018.
11. WHYY 2012.
12. Dance 2017.
13. US Census Bureau.
14. Abramitzky, Boustan, and Eriksson 2014; Borjas 1989.
15. Pew Charitable Trusts 2018; Deto 2017; O'Dea 2019.
16. Gilsinan 2013; Vishwanath 2018.
17. Margolis 2018.
18. McCabe 2012.
19. Krogstad 2019.
20. Cwiek 2016.
21. Guerrieri, Hartley, and Hurst 2013.
22. Wheeler and Cox 2013.
23. Awad 2018.
24. Wood 2019.
25. Albouy, Christensen, and Sarmiento-Barbieri 2020.
26. Kleiman and Saiger 1990.
27. Duncan 2018.

8

New Knowledge Fuels the Comeback

Millions of people continue to live in Baltimore, Cleveland, Detroit, Philadelphia, Pittsburgh, and St. Louis. These cities have bad winters, hundreds of thousands of people lacking a good education and human capital, and old run-down buildings. Each of these cities is situated close to bodies of water but is scarred from years of underinvestment. Within these cities, many neighborhoods feature cheap rents, which act as a poverty magnet. Big pockets of poverty not only create recurrent intergenerational poverty but also make it difficult to finance significant investment in public goods through tax dollars. This in turn causes many people who succeed in these cities to leave once they can. It also means that wealthy and educated people are less likely to move to these cities because of their lower quality of life.

This book has covered the causes of urban poverty in these cities and the consequences of this poverty for attracting jobs and growing the population. We have analyzed the specific challenges these cities face and have suggested pathways for making progress. We do not have a formula for guaranteeing shared urban prosperity. Rather, we have stressed the importance of experimentation and formal evaluation to learn what works. Neither the state nor the federal government has displayed an eagerness to invest large sums of money in renovating these cities. Given this reality, these cities must figure out how to configure the "rules of the game"—in order to create more prosperity, invest in the up-and-coming generation, and attract and retain footloose people and firms from elsewhere.

Urban economic research emphasizes that places matter in shaping economic and social mobility. We have argued that poor people are poor in part because they live near other poor people. Many non-poor people are comfortable with this arrangement, have pushed for it politically, and have voted with their feet to make it a reality. Rich people choose to live in cities and neighborhoods with the highest quality of life, while poor people can only afford to live in cities and neighborhoods with low quality of life. A key issue is whether this is a selection effect (because poor people cannot afford the rent in better areas) or a treatment effect (because poverty has the effect of raising local crime and lowering local public school quality). Such a treatment effect would mean that a by-product of the poor clustering together is a downward spiral that further increases inequality. Children are more likely to achieve their full potential if they grow up in good neighborhoods. Mixed-income neighborhoods pose a possible solution to this problem, but wealthy people are resistant to this and have been increasingly isolating themselves in recent decades.

A source of tension brought up throughout this book is where poor people live within cities. Most non-poor people do not want to live near the poor, and most cities do not welcome poor individuals. Many local policies, such as zoning with a minimum lot size, a reluctance to accept people using vouchers to pay their rent, and federal policies such as the construction of isolated public housing, are ways to concentrate the poor and effectively create a moat separating them from the non-poor. Isolating the urban poor increases the likelihood that they will remain poor because of bad schools, a lack of information and knowledge about jobs, exposure to polluted environments, the influence of peers who do not work, and exposure to crime—all of which raise the likelihood of intergenerational poverty. A troubling trade-off emerges. If the poor are isolated, the non-poor gain in the short run, but the children of the poor and the rest of society bear medium-term costs resulting from this isolation. In an economy where people fear crime and worry that poor people commit the bulk of it, efforts to reduce crime impose costs on the poor and hinder income growth and racial integration.

Competition for the Mobile Tax Base

The combined population of the six cities is tiny compared with the entire population of the United States. For these cities to grow, they must do a better job of retaining their current residents and attracting outsiders to move there. Given the competition for attracting skilled workers, people will move to these center cities only if they offer a mix of good wages, low taxes, and a high quality of life relative to rival cities. Street safety plays a central role. Fear of violence creates an incentive for the footloose to distance themselves from those they fear. Whether fair or not, wealthy people can vote with their feet and have many options of where to live. Likewise, footloose firms will be more likely to move to these cities if they feature low taxes and a high-quality workforce. Philadelphia and Pittsburgh have made progress on these fronts.

A major theme of this book has been the positive synergies between the private sector's investment and the public sector's ability to deliver quality local public services. Consider the relationship between urban street safety and real estate investment. In areas where people feel safe, they spend more time outdoors shopping and visiting. This provides an incentive for real estate owners and developers to upgrade buildings and compete for more business. As crime is reduced, more businesses want to locate in a city, and more money is available to invest in education as police and prison budgets are reduced. Investments in education, skills formation, entrepreneurship, and business development can act as incentives for people who might otherwise turn to a life of crime to pay the bills.

Expectations play a key role in determining whether a place makes a comeback. Urban economists have examined how places recover from major shocks such as bombings during wartime and major fires. As was the case for Boston after the fire of 1872, Japan after World War II, Dresden after its firebombing, cities bombed during the Vietnam War, and New York City after 9/11, people believed that the fundamentals of these areas remained strong, and an enormous investment of capital followed. These case studies highlight the importance of expectations.

If everyone in the United States becomes optimistic about Cleveland's future, people would visit the city more and some would move there. This would boost aggregate demand, raise local real estate prices, and rejuvenate the city. Expectations also matter in shaping investment patterns. If young people whose parents live in poverty do not expect to live to age 50, why would they pay attention in high school? If real estate investors believe that crime will remain high in certain neighborhoods, why would they purchase aging properties there and redevelop them?

How do different people form expectations that an area will enjoy a comeback? During a time of considerable political polarization, who has the trust and the credibility to make the case that one of our six cities is on the rise? Given the salience of crime, one possibility is that if each of our cities enjoyed a 90 percent reduction in its murder rate (similar to what Los Angeles and New York City achieved over the last few decades), this clear evidence of progress in street safety would drive other major changes.

History and Expectations

While expectations play an important role in determining the future of people and places, so too does history. In his 2011 book *Triumph of the City*, Edward Glaeser argues that Detroit's failure to maintain its economic place of prominence is due to a combination of historic factors. The city's reliance on a handful of large industrial manufacturers like Ford instead of a thriving small-business ecosystem and its overwhelming stock of durable capital in the form of vacant homes and infrastructure built for another age have held it back in recent decades.[1]

In his 1991 article "History versus Expectations," Nobel laureate economist Paul Krugman lays out the competing forces of history and expectations.[2] History sets the preconditions that determine a city's physical look and feel at any point in time based on its residents' past choices, while expectations play a central role in determining future investment patterns. Krugman emphasizes the possibility of a type of self-fulfilling prophecy. The slower the rate that an economy adjusts, the more history matters, as it will be both costly and risky to move quickly. If change is rapid, then expectations will win, as slow movers lose out.

The fall and recent rise of Baltimore's Pennsylvania Avenue offers one relevant example. In the 1950s, Pennsylvania Avenue was the economic and cultural heart of Black Baltimore, regularly featuring jazz legends Billie Holiday, Miles Davis, and John Coltrane, while being home to the first Black-owned and operated hospital, first Black-owned movie theatre, and first Black male social club in the city. Perhaps nowhere in the city was hit harder by the 1968 riots, as the avenue experienced economic decline and became a haven for crime and drug dealing in the 1970s and 1980s. In 2015, the avenue was ground zero for the unrest that followed the death of Freddie Gray while in police custody. But by 2020, local advocates ran a successful grassroots campaign to have the avenue designated as the state's first ever Black arts and entertainment district, and investment followed. After shifting the narrative and changing expectations for the area, developers began building new apartment complexes nearby.

Throughout this book, we have discussed the importance of both history and expectations in the context of the future of the six cities we study. The cities all struggle with an industrial history of environmental pollution from factories in the form of lead and other heavy metals, a history of redlining and racial housing policies that resulted in a disinvestment in Black communities, a history of a durable housing stock built to house hundreds of thousands more residents, a history of underinvestment in public schools and early childhood education, and a history of mass incarceration that punished poor Blacks for minor drug offenses.

The slow progress that the six cities have made in reversing this history means they have become stuck in place in many ways. A coordination failure has occurred, as few have been willing to be a first mover in investing. In aggregate, this lowers total investment and reduces the likelihood of future success. But history does not have to be determinative. If our cities are able to make impactful investments in people and neighborhoods, then residents and firms would follow suit, guided by a belief that there is a bright future ahead.

The Grand Bargain

Suppose these cities reduce their crime and experience a boom. As local communities enjoy an improvement in their quality of life, how much do rents rise? Who gains from the upgrades in the quality of life? While we do not fully understand the causes of major city crime declines, such progress sets off a type of domino effect. As a city becomes safer, people spend more time in public spaces and walk the streets at night. This in turn provides an incentive for retailers and cultural outlets to compete for their share of the emerging consumer city.[3]

As these cities enjoy greater economic success, the tax revenue in these cities will increase. This will allow the cities to finance poverty reduction policies, ranging from removing lead in older housing to improving early education for young children. In 2016, for example, New York City mayor Bill de Blasio dedicated a large share of the gentrification windfall from the rise of property taxes to pay for prekindergarten for all.

Building the skills of young people through long-term, targeted, research-informed investments will lead to improved human capital. This will result in improved economic outcomes and mobility, less spending on welfare programs, and less spending on punitive government programs. As urbanites enjoy greater shared prosperity, a safer city emerges, and real estate investors have strong incentives to invest in neighborhoods that they had previously viewed as too risky and unprofitable.

We are cautiously optimistic that our six cities can identify strategies to reduce their murder rates. This will create a virtuous circle. There will be more hope for poor residents, which will entice some of the mobile tax base to live, work, and play inside city limits. This will generate more tax revenue for the important human and health capital interventions that are needed. The key unknown is the urban governance factor. As discussed in chapter six, the public sector has insufficient accountability and innovation to allow voters to recognize and credibly address inefficiency in delivering public services.

During a time of great concern about income inequality, key distributional issues arise. As quality of life improves in neighborhoods, will rents soar? A standard economic prescription is to change local zoning laws to allow real estate developers to build more housing in increasingly desirable areas. For example, so-called upzoning would allow multi-family apartment buildings to be built, which could house both poorer and wealthier city residents. In booming cities such as Portland and Seattle, the combination of rising demand and limits to new housing supply have translated into soaring rents, which have displaced poor renters from their neighborhoods. Whether our six cities can avoid these housing challenges remains an open question.

Benchmarks of Urban Progress

Back in the mid-1970s, few New Yorkers could have imagined the rise of Manhattan to what it now has become. Back then, prime real estate was relatively cheap.[4] While New York City's recent rise does not guarantee Detroit's comeback, it does serve as an inspirational case study. New York City's weather has not improved; instead the city's rise has been predicated on improvements in quality of life (caused by reduced crime and increased environmental investments) and a boom in its main industries (finance and information technology). Urban economists tend to use home price dynamics to measure a city's or a neighborhood's well-being. If real estate prices are rising in such an area, this signals that some combination of local economic growth and local quality of life is improving.

In this age of big data, with ongoing improvements in urban data collection and distribution, an increasing number of relevant benchmarks are available for judging whether shared progress is taking place. Crime data can reveal which dangerous neighborhoods are becoming safer. New restaurant openings and new building permits suggest which communities are on the rise. Across our six cities, are more young people achieving their full potential based on economic outcomes such as employment and earnings? Are young people enjoying gains in terms of improved health? These indicators are perhaps the most important measures for the future of our cities. They signal to the world how our cities treat and respect the new generation.

The six cities compete with the rest of the United States for footloose workers and firms. In the near future, will more skilled outsiders move to the six cities? Will more great firms move to their center cities? Will more start-up firms thrive? Will any of our six cities develop a reputation as a hotbed of innovation? These will be market tests of whether these cities are catching up with the rest of urban America.

A Research Agenda for the 21st-Century City

Raj Chetty and his team at Opportunity Insights have shown that our cities are not places that promote upward economic and social mobility. As we highlighted at the beginning of this book, 98 percent of all counties in the United States have higher economic mobility rates than Baltimore City. Within our cities, specific neighborhoods struggle with seemingly intractable cycles of intergenerational poverty. In cities like New York City, neighborhoods that were struggling in the 1970s are now thriving. Critics would quickly point out that, because of migration, such place-based progress may mask continued poverty for the children of the original poor residents who are not able to afford the rising rents. Research on urban upward mobility must track people and places over time.

An ambitious urban social science agenda, done in partnership with communities, should include five areas of research. First, social scientists must seek to understand what safety and policing interventions can lead to reductions in violent crime. The era of mass incarceration seems to be coming to a close, and new solutions to violent crime, such as cognitive behavioral therapy and job interventions, are being promoted. We need more research on the costs and benefits of this programming and how government agencies can collaborate with service providers to target these interventions effectively and efficiently at those who need them the most. We need to highlight what works in creating safe communities so that children do not grow up traumatized.

Second, we need to understand why our urban public school systems are falling behind the national average. What innovations in education can help children reach their full potential? Who chooses to be a public school teacher in these cities? Are they incentivized to build up their skills? What flexibility do the school principals have in experimenting with different learning formats? Do charter schools and school choice raise the game for other schools or simply siphon off the best students? We need more evaluation and testing of what works and what doesn't work in our cities if we are to educate the next generation of successful leaders and entrepreneurs.

Third, we need to identify barriers to entrepreneurship and small-business growth to make sure that our young children see an avenue to a rewarding career. How could improving access to capital and creating new avenues to business financing help underperforming businesses grow? What role do technical assistance and business services play in training and improving the skills of local entrepreneurs? How important is the local entrepreneurial environment to the success of a business? We need much more research on the local context of entrepreneurs in our cities to understand the dynamics of business and job growth.

Fourth, we need to encourage the development of new housing in areas of the city whose fundamentals are improving on account of environmental progress, reductions in local crime, and improvements in local public transit. What options do our cities have for upzoning and getting rid of minimum lot size requirements? What role do Section 8 vouchers have in deconcentrating poverty and improving upward mobility? How can cities work with neighborhoods to improve the siting of public housing units so that they are not only located in poor communities? What role can community land trusts play in protecting and creating permanently affordable housing units? How can cities use transit-oriented development to ensure that housing is connected to labor markets?

Finally, we need to better understand the risk of future environmental threats and determine how we can protect the most vulnerable in our communities. Climate change is a growing threat, but we are only beginning to understand the disparate impact that flooding, air pollution, extreme heat, and other environmental threats have on different neighborhoods and different people. Furthermore, we are only beginning to understand how people adapt to changing risk scenarios and what protective measures they put in place. We need to better understand how cities, homeowners, and businesses can adapt to a changing world.

For our cities to improve their quality of life and economic and social mobility outcomes for all their residents, leaders need to be more open to innovation and experimentation. They need to be honest about failure and open to constructive evaluation and criticism. We need honest conversations about what has and has not worked.

A Brighter Future

In our era of big data, urban data collection and reporting can measure important indicators of economic and quality-of-life dynamics. Our research center at Johns Hopkins University, the 21st Century Cities Initiative, studies these data as we work collaboratively with local governments and urban businesses to assess the challenges and opportunities offered in different cities. We know that we do not have the answer to every issue faced by the six cities we discussed in this book. However, as we have emphasized throughout this book, the pathway to success is to adopt the mindset of a clinical physician. Doctors provide a diagnosis and then consider a variety of treatments, while being aware of the possible side effects and unintended consequences. Doctors and medical researchers have the advantage of being able to run controlled clinical trials, showing the effect of a treatment across hundreds of patients. Running a similar experiment in a city is difficult but not impossible, and a center like ours is here to help.

The pathways we have sketched out in this book offer a constructive approach for how local officials, business leaders, citizens, and academics can work together to accelerate our cities' comeback. The steps taken today will lay the groundwork for the future trajectories of these cities.

NOTES

1. Glaeser 2011.
2. Krugman 1991.
3. Glaeser, Kolko, and Saiz 2001.
4. Furman Center 2008.

References

Abdulkadiroğlu A, Pathak P, Walters C. 2018. Free to choose: Can school choice reduce student achievement? American Economic Journal: Applied Economics 10 (1): 175–206.

Abramitzky R, Boustan LP, Eriksson K. 2014. A nation of immigrants: Assimilation and economic outcomes in the age of mass migration. Journal of Political Economy 122 (3): 467–506.

Abt T. 2019. Bleeding Out: The Devastating Consequences of Urban Violence—and a Bold New Plan for Peace in the Streets. Hachette.

Ackerman B, Alstott A. 1999. The Stakeholder Society. Yale University Press.

Addo FR, Sassler S, Williams K. 2016. Reexamining the association of maternal age and marital status at first birth with youth educational attainment. Journal of Marriage and Family 78 (5): 1252–1268.

Agan A, Starr S. 2018. Ban the box, criminal records, and racial discrimination: A field experiment. Quarterly Journal of Economics 133 (1): 191–235.

Akbar PA, Li S, Shertzer A, Walsh RP. 2019. Racial Segregation in Housing Markets and the Erosion of Black Wealth. National Bureau of Economic Research Working Paper No. 25805. Cambridge, MA: NBER.

Albouy D, Christensen P, Sarmiento-Barbieri I. 2020. Unlocking amenities: Estimating public good complementarity. Journal of Public Economics 182 (February): 104110.

Alchian AA, Kessel RA. 1962. Competition, monopoly, and the pursuit of pecuniary gain. In: Aspects of Labor Economics (pp. 157–183). Princeton University Press.

Alesina A, Baqir R, Easterly W. 2000. Redistributive public employment. Journal of Urban Economics 48 (2): 219–241.

Alesina A, Danninger S, Rostagno M. 2001. Redistribution through public employment: The case of Italy. International Monetary Fund Staff Papers 48 (3): 447–473.

Alesina A, Glaeser E. 2004. Fighting Poverty in the US and Europe: A World of Difference. Oxford University Press.

Alon T, Doepke M, Olmstead-Rumsey J, Tertilt M. 2020. The Impact of COVID-19 on Gender Equality. National Bureau of Economic Research Working Paper No. 26947. Cambridge, MA: NBER.

Amsden D. 2017. How Baltimore quietly became the East Coast's next cool city. Smithsonian Magazine, July 31.

Anderson J. 2020. Maryland laws that have long protected police face scrutiny as public demands more accountability. Baltimore Sun, June 12.

Anderson P. 2010. Child care. In: Levine P, Zimmerman D (Eds.). Targeting Investments in Children: Fighting Poverty When Resources Are Limited (pp. 59–76). University of Chicago Press.

Andes S, Horowitz M, Helwig R, Katz B. 2017. Capturing the Next Economy: Pittsburgh's Rise as a Global Innovation City. Brookings Institution.

Austin B, Glaeser E, Summers LH. 2018. Saving the heartland: Place-based policies in 21st century America. Brookings Papers on Economic Activity, Spring, 151–255.

Autor D. 2019. Work of the Past, Work of the Future. National Bureau of Economic Research Working Paper No. 25588. Cambridge, MA: NBER.

Autor D, Dorn D, Hanson G. 2018. When work disappears: Manufacturing decline and the falling marriage-market value of young men. American Economic Review: Insights 1 (2): 161–178.

Autor DH, Dorn D, Hanson GH. 2013. The China syndrome: Local labor market effects of import competition in the United States. American Economic Review 103 (6): 2121–2168.

Autor DH, Duggan MG. 2003. The rise in the disability rolls and the decline in unemployment. Quarterly Journal of Economics 118 (1): 157–206.

Awad AM. 2018. Where does all the marijuana money go? Colorado's pot taxes, explained. CPR News, October 22.

Babcock S. 2018. Port Covington developers plan to build "Cyber Town, USA," announce first three tenants. Technical.ly Baltimore, October 18.

Badger E, Bui Q. 2020. Riots long ago, luxury living today. New York Times, July 10.

Bahaj S, Foulis A, Pinter G. 2020. Home values and firm behavior. American Economic Review 110 (7): 2225–2270.

Baltimore City Bureau of the Budget and Management Research. Fiscal 2020: Summary of the Adopted Budget, p. 149. https://bbmr.baltimorecity.gov/sites/default/files/Final%20SOTA%20FY20-compressed%20web.pdf.

Baltimore City Department of Finance. 2018. Report on Overtime at the Baltimore Police Department. https://finance.baltimorecity.gov/sites/default/files/Report.%20Overtime%20at%20BPD.Final_.v.1.pdf.

Baltimore City Health Department. Baltimore City's Response to the Opioid Epidemic. Accessed July 18, 2020. https://health.baltimorecity.gov/opioid-overdose/baltimore-city-overdose-prevention-and-response-information.

Baltimore City Health Department. 2011. Neighborhood Health Profile.

Baltimore Development Corporation. Brownfields Tax Credit. Accessed July 18, 2020. http://baltimoredevelopment.com/incentives/brownfields/.

Bartik TJ. 2019. Should Place-Based Jobs Policies Be Used to Help Distressed Communities? Upjohn Institute Working Paper No. 19-308.

Baum-Snow N. 2007. Did highways cause suburbanization? Quarterly Journal of Economics 122 (2): 775–805.

Baum-Snow N, Hartley D. 2020. Accounting for central neighborhood change, 1980–2010. Journal of Urban Economics 117 (May): 103228.

Bayer P, Fang H, McMillan R. 2014. Separate when equal? Racial inequality and residential segregation. Journal of Urban Economics 82 (July): 32–48.

Becker G. 1968. Crime and punishment: An economic approach. Journal of Political Economy 76 (2): 169–217.

Becker GS, Murphy KM. 1988. A theory of rational addiction. Journal of Political Economy 96 (4): 675–700.

Bell A, Chetty R, Jaravel X, Petkova N, Van Reenen J. 2017. Who Becomes an Inventor in America? The Importance of Exposure to Innovation. Centre for Economic Performance Discussion Paper No 1519.

Bergman P, Chetty R, DeLuca S, Hendren N, Katz LF, Palmer C. 2019. Creating Moves to Opportunity: Experimental Evidence on Barriers to Neighborhood Choice. National Bureau of Economic Research Working Paper No. 26164. Cambridge, MA: NBER.

Bertrand M, Mullainathan S. 2001. Are CEOs rewarded for luck? The ones without principals are. Quarterly Journal of Economics 116 (3): 901–932.

Bertrand M, Mullainathan S. 2004. Are Emily and Greg more employable than Lakisha and Jamal? A field experiment on labor market discrimination. American Economic Review 94 (4): 991–1013.

Borjas GJ. 1989. Immigrant and emigrant earnings: A longitudinal study. Economic Inquiry 27 (1): 21–37.

Boustan LP. 2016. Competition in the Promised Land: Black Migrants in Northern Cities and Labor Markets. Princeton University Press.

Bowen D, Kisida B. 2019. Investigating Causal Effects of Arts Education Experiences: Experimental Evidence from Houston's Arts Access Initiative. Rice University's Kinder Institute for Urban Research.

Branas C, South E, Kondo M, Hohl B, Bourgois P, Wiebe D, MacDonald J. 2018. Citywide cluster randomized trial to restore blighted vacant land and its effects on violence, crime, and fear. Proceedings of the National Academy of Sciences 115 (12): 2946–2951.

Breckenridge Capital Advisors. 2020. 2020 Municipal Credit Outlook.

Breitenstein S, Gross D, Fogg L, Ridge A, Garvey C, Julion W, Tucker S. 2012. The Chicago Parent Program: Comparing 1-year outcomes for African American and Latino parents of young children. Research in Nursing and Health 35 (5): 475–489.

Brinkman J, Lin J. 2019. Freeway Revolts! The Quality of Life Effects of Highways. Federal Reserve Bank of Philadelphia Working Paper 19-29.

Burdick-Will J, Stein M, Grigg J. 2019. Danger on the way to school: Exposure to violent crime, public transportation, and absenteeism. Sociological Science 6 (February): 118–142.

Busso M, Gregory J, Kline P. 2013. Assessing the incidence and efficiency of a prominent place based policy. American Economic Review 103 (2): 897–947.

Cameron SV, Heckman JJ. 2001. The dynamics of educational attainment for Black, Hispanic, and white males. Journal of Political Economy 109 (3): 455–499.

Card D, Mas A, Rothstein J. 2008. Tipping and the dynamics of segregation. Quarterly Journal of Economics 123 (1): 177–218.

Carter WH, Schill MH, Wachter SM. 1998. Polarisation, public housing and racial minorities in US cities. Urban Studies 35 (10): 1889–1911.

Chang HF, Sigman H. 2000. Incentives to settle under joint and several liability: An empirical analysis of superfund litigation. Journal of Legal Studies 29 (1): 205–236.

Charles K, Guryan J. 2008. Prejudice and wages: An empirical assessment of Becker's *The Economics of Discrimination*. Journal of Political Economy 116 (5): 773–809.

Charter School Performance in Maryland. 2019. Center for Research on Education Outcomes, Stanford University.

Chen H, Gompers P, Kovner A, Lerner J. 2010. Buy local? The geography of venture capital. Journal of Urban Economics 67 (1): 90–102.

Chetty R, Hendren N. 2018. The impacts of neighborhoods on intergenerational mobility I: Childhood exposure effects. Quarterly Journal of Economics 133 (3): 1107–1162.

Chetty R, Hendren N, Katz LF. 2016. The effects of exposure to better neighborhoods on children: New evidence from the Moving to Opportunity experiment. American Economic Review 106 (4): 855–902.

Christensen P, Sarmiento-Barbieri I, Timmins C. 2020. Housing Discrimination and the Toxics Exposure Gap in the United States: Evidence from the Rental Market. National Bureau of Economic Research Working Paper No. 26805. Cambridge, MA: NBER.

Christensen P, Timmins C. 2018. Sorting or Steering: Experimental Evidence on the Economic Effects of Housing Discrimination. National Bureau of Economic Research Working Paper No. 24826. Cambridge, MA: NBER.

Chyn E. 2018. Moved to opportunity: The long-run effects of public housing demolition on children. American Economic Review 108 (10): 3028–3056.

City News Service. 2018. Program pays San Diego homeless minimum wage for trash pickup. KPBS, February 26.

City of St. Louis, Department of Health. 2018. Childhood Lead Poisoning in the City of St. Louis: Annual Report.

Clay K, Jones R. 2008. Migrating to riches? Evidence from the California gold rush. Journal of Economic History 68 (4): 997–1027.

Collins WJ, Margo RA. 2007. The economic aftermath of the 1960s riots in American cities: Evidence from property values. Journal of Economic History 67 (4): 849–883.

Condliffe B, Boyd M, DeLuca S. 2015. Stuck in school: How social context shapes school choice for inner-city students. Teachers College Record 117 (3): 1–36.

Conklin J, Ambrose B, Lopez L. 2019. Preferential Treatment in Financial Contracts: Does Borrower and Broker Race Affect Mortgage Prices. Working paper from the Social Science Research Network, http://dx.doi.org/10.2139/ssrn.3006793.

Cornish S. 2014. Black voter turnout staggeringly low in Baltimore City. Afro News, November 12.

Costa DL, Kahn ME. 2000. Power couples: Changes in the locational choice of the college educated, 1940–1990. Quarterly Journal of Economics 115 (4): 1287–1315.

Cummings JL, DiPasquale D, Kahn ME. 2002. Measuring the consequences of promoting inner city homeownership. Journal of Housing Economics 11 (4): 330–359.

Currie J, Davis L, Greenstone M, Walker R. 2015. Environmental health risks and housing values: Evidence from 1,600 toxic plant openings and closings. American Economic Review 105 (2): 678–709.

Currie J, Zivin JG, Mullins J, Neidell M. 2014. What do we know about short-and long-term effects of early-life exposure to pollution? Annual Review of Resource Economics 6 (1): 217–247.

Cutler DM, Glaeser EL. 1997. Are ghettos good or bad? Quarterly Journal of Economics 112 (3): 827–872.
Cutler DM, Glaeser EL, Vigdor JL. 1999. The rise and decline of the American ghetto. Journal of Political Economy 107 (3): 455–506.
Cuyahoga County Board of Health. Annual Reports of Confirmed Elevated Blood Lead Levels for Children Residing in the City of Cleveland. Reports available from 2004 to 2017. https://www.ccbh.net/lead-level-maps/.
Cwiek S. 2016 Detroit's immigrant population trends up. Michigan Radio, October 31.
Dance S. 2017. Baltimore officials approve $1.6 billion, 13-year sewer repair plan. Baltimore Sun, August 9.
Davis R. 2005. Study: 1 in 5 young black city men in jail. Baltimore Sun, March 15.
Dennis S, Selway W. 2020. McConnell says he favors letting states declare bankruptcy. Bloomberg News, April 22.
Derenoncourt E. 2019. Can You Move to Opportunity? Evidence from the Great Migration. Working paper, https://scholar.harvard.edu/elloraderenoncourt/publications/can-you-move-opportunity-evidence-great-migration-job-market-paper.
Deto R. 2017. Immigrants are propping up the Pittsburgh metro area population. Pittsburgh City Paper, June 7.
Detroit Coalition for Economic Inclusion. Black Business Owner Economic Confidence Survey. https://nationalbusinessleague.org/ncei/.
Dingel J, Neiman B. 2020. How Many Jobs Can Be Done at Home? National Bureau of Economic Research Working Paper No. 26948. Cambridge, MA: NBER.
DiPasquale D, Glaeser EL. 1998. The Los Angeles riot and the economics of urban unrest. Journal of Urban Economics 43 (1): 52–78.
DiSalvo D. 2015. Government against Itself: Public Union Power and Its Consequences. Oxford University Press.
Doleac JL, Hansen B. 2017. Moving to job opportunities? The effect of "ban the box" on the composition of cities. American Economic Review 107 (5): 556–559.
Dumais G, Ellison G, Glaeser EL. 2002. Geographic concentration as a dynamic process. Review of Economics and Statistics 84 (2): 193–204.
DuPuis N, Langan T, McFarland C, Panettieri A, Rainwater B. 2018. City Rights in an Era of Preemption: A State-by-State Analysis, 2018 Update. National League of Cities.
Durham R, Connolly F. 2016. Baltimore Community Schools: Promise & Progress. Baltimore Education Research Consortium.
Durham R, Stein M, Connolly F. 2015. College Opportunities and Success: Baltimore City Graduates through the Class of 2014. Baltimore Education Research Consortium.
Durlauf SN. 2012. Poverty traps and Appalachia. In: Appalachian Legacy: Economic Opportunity after the War on Poverty (pp. 169–206). Brookings Institution Press.
Durlauf SN, Ioannides YM. 2010. Social interactions. Annual Review of Economics 2: 451–478.
Dworak L. 2019. Scaling Workforce Development Programming in Baltimore. Abell Foundation.

Economy League of Greater Philadelphia. 2017. Industry Analytics for the City of Philadelphia's Workforce Strategy.

Edin K. 2000. What do low-income single mothers say about marriage? Social Problems 47 (1): 112–133.

Eichensehr M. 2019. Baltimore software firm Fearless launches new business incubator. Baltimore Business Journal, May 9.

Emer L, Kalkbrenner, O'Brien A, Yan M, Cisler RA, Weinhardt L. 2020. Association of childhood blood lead levels with firearm violence perpetration and victimization in Milwaukee. Environmental Research 180 (January): 108822.

Fairlie R, Robb A, Robinson D. 2009. Patterns of Financing: A Comparison between White- and African-American Young Firms—Fourth in a Series of Reports Using Data from the Kauffman Firm Survey. Kauffman Foundation Firm Survey Research.

Fairlie R, Robb A, Robinson D. 2016. Black and White: Access to Capital among Minority-Owned Startups. Stanford Institute for Economic Policy Reseaerch Discussion Paper No. 17-03.

Feuer A. 2013. The mayor's geek squad. New York Times, March 23.

Feyrer J, Mansur ET, Sacerdote B. 2017. Geographic dispersion of economic shocks: Evidence from the fracking revolution. American Economic Review 107 (4): 1313–1334.

Feyrer J, Sacerdote B, Stern AD. 2007. Did the Rust Belt become shiny? A study of cities and counties that lost steel and auto jobs in the 1980s. Brookings-Wharton Papers on Urban Affairs, January 1, 41–102.

Fire and Police Employees' Retirement System of the City of Baltimore. 2019. Actuarial Valuation Report as of June 30, 2019. https://publicplansdata.org/reports/MD_BALTIMORECITY-PFP_AV_2019_155.pdf.

Fischel WA. 2009. The Homevoter Hypothesis: How Home Values Influence Local Government Taxation, School Finance, and Land-Use Policies. Harvard University Press.

Florida R. 2014. The Rise of the Creative Class—Revisited. Revised and expanded ed. Basic Books.

Florida R. 2017. The New Urban Crisis. Basic Books.

Florida R. 2019. Maps reveal where the creative class is growing. Bloomberg CityLab, July 9.

Furman Center. 2008. Trends in New York City housing price appreciation In: State of New York City's Housing and Neighborhoods (pp. 9–25). https://furmancenter.org/files/sotc/State_of_the_City_2008.pdf.

García JL, Heckman JJ, Leaf DE, Prados MJ. 2017. Quantifying the Life-Cycle Benefits of a Prototypical Early Childhood Program. National Bureau of Economic Research Working Paper No. 23479. Cambridge, MA: NBER.

Gaspar J, Glaeser EL. 1998. Information technology and the future of cities. Journal of Urban Economics 43 (1): 136–156.

Gershenson S, Hart C, Hyman J, Lindsay C, Papageorge NW. 2018. The Long-Run Impacts of Same-Race Teachers. National Bureau of Economic Research Working Paper No. 25254. Cambridge, MA: NBER.

Gertler P, Heckman J, Pinto R, Zanolini A, Vermeerch C, Walker S, Chang SM, Grantham-McGregor S. 2014. Labor market returns to an early childhood stimulation intervention in Jamaica. Science 344 (6187): 998–1001.

Gibson-Davis C, Edin K, McLanahan S. 2005. High hopes but even higher expectations: The retreat from marriage among low-income couples. Journal of Marriage and Family 67 (5): 1301–1312.

Gilsinan, K. 2013. Why are there so many Bosnians in St. Louis? Bloomberg CityLab, February 15.

Glaeser E. 2011. Triumph of the City. Pan Macmillan.

Glaeser E, Sunstein, C. 2014. How to deregulate cities and states. Wall Street Journal, August 24.

Glaeser EL. 2000. Cities and ethics: An essay for Jane Jacobs. Journal of Urban Affairs 22 (4): 473–493.

Glaeser EL. 2015. A new urban opportunity agenda. City Journal, Autumn.

Glaeser EL. 2020. Urbanization and Its Discontents. National Bureau of Economic Research Working Paper No. 26839. Cambridge, MA: NBER.

Glaeser EL, Gyourko J. 2005. Urban decline and durable housing. Journal of Political Economy 113 (2): 345–375.

Glaeser EL, Gyourko J, Saks R. 2005. Why is Manhattan so expensive? Regulation and the rise in housing prices. Journal of Law and Economics 48 (2): 331–369.

Glaeser EL, Kolko J, Saiz A. 2001. Consumer city. Journal of Economic Geography 1 (1): 27–50.

Glaeser EL, Ponzetto GA, Tobio K. 2014. Cities, skills and regional change. Regional Studies 48 (1): 7–43.

Glaeser EL, Rosenthal S, Strange W. 2009. Urban Economics and Entrepreneurship. National Bureau of Economic Research Working Paper No. 15536. Cambridge, MA: NBER.

Goldstein S, McMullen K. 2018. Fact Check: A Survey of Available Data on Juvenile Crime in Baltimore City. Abell Report 31 (3): 1–15.

Gomez-Ibanez J, Meyer JR. 2011 Going Private: The International Experience with Transport Privatization. Brookings Institution Press.

Goodman, L. 2018. A closer look at the fifteen-year drop in black homeownership. Urban Institute Urban Wire, February 13.

Gormley Jr WT, Phillips D, Anderson S. 2018. The effects of Tulsa's pre-K program on middle school student performance. Journal of Policy Analysis and Management 37 (1): 63–87.

Government Innovators Network. CitiStat. Harvard Kennedy School Ash Center for Democratic Governance and Innovation. Accessed July 18, 2020. https://www.innovations.harvard.edu/citistat.

Graff Zivin J, Neidell M. 2013. Environment, health, and human capital. Journal of Economic Literature 51 (3): 689–730.

Greenlee A. 2019. Assessing the intersection of neighborhood change and residential mobility pathways for the Chicago metropolitan area (2006–2015). Housing Policy Debate 29 (1): 186–212.

Gross D, Garvey C, Julion W, Fogg L, Tucker S, Mokros H. 2009. Efficacy of the Chicago Parent Program with low-income African American and Latino parents of young children. Preventative Science 10 (1): 54–65.

Guerrieri V, Hartley D, Hurst E. 2013. Endogenous gentrification and housing price dynamics. Journal of Public Economics 100 (April 1): 45–60.

Gupta A, Nieuwerburgh SV, Kontokosta C. 2020. Take the Q Train: Value Capture of Public Infrastructure Projects. National Bureau of Economic Research Working Paper No. 26789. Cambridge, MA: NBER.

Gyourko J, Mayer C, Sinai T. 2013. Superstar cities. American Economic Journal: Economic Policy 5 (4): 167–199.

Gyourko J, Summers A. 1997. A New Strategy for Helping Cities Pay for the Poor. Brookings Institution.

Handbury J, Weinstein DE. 2014. Goods prices and availability in cities. Review of Economic Studies 82 (1): 258–296.

Hanson A, Rohlin S. 2013. Do spatially targeted redevelopment programs spillover? Regional Science and Urban Economics 43 (1): 86–100.

Heckman JJ. 1994. Is job training oversold? Public Interest, no. 115: 91–115.

Heckman Equation. 2014. Professor Heckman on the State of the Union Address. https://heckmanequation.org/resource/professor-heckman-on-the-state-of-the-union-address/.

Hellerstein JK, Neumark D, McInerney M. 2008. Spatial mismatch or racial mismatch? Journal of Urban Economics 64 (2): 464–479.

Hershbein B, Kahn L. 2018. Do recessions accelerate routine-biased technological change? Evidence from vacancy postings. American Economic Review 108 (7): 1737–1772.

Hirschman AO. 1970. Exit, Voice, and Loyalty: Responses to Decline in Firms, Organizations, and States. Harvard University Press.

Holian M, Kahn, ME. 2015. Household carbon emissions from driving and center city quality of life. Ecological Economics 116: 362–368.

Horowitz J, Carlock A. 2017. Juvenile commitment rate falls by half nationally in 10 years. Pew Charitable Trusts, September 18.

Houston Community Data Connections. 2018. Tracking eighth-graders' postsecondary outcomes in Harris County. Rice University's Kinder Institute for Urban Research.

Howell O. 2018. Philadelphia's Poor: Experience from Below the Poverty Line. Pew Charitable Trusts. https://www.pewtrusts.org/-/media/assets/2018/09/phillypovertyreport2018.pdf.

Hoxby CM. 2000. Does competition among public schools benefit students and taxpayers? American Economic Review 90 (5): 1209–1238.

Hoynes H, Patel A. 2018. Effective policy for reducing poverty and inequality? The earned income tax credit and the distribution of income. Journal of Human Resources 53 (4): 859–890.

Ideas42. 2017. CBT 2.0 User's Manual. http://www.ideas42.org/wp-content/uploads/2017/01/CBTCurriculum.pdf.

Institute of Museum and Library Services. 2018. https://www.imls.gov/.

Ioannides YM, Loury LD. 2004. Job information networks, neighborhood effects, and inequality. Journal of Economic Literature 42 (4): 1056–1093.

Jacob BA, Ludwig J, Miller DL. 2013 The effects of housing and neighborhood conditions on child mortality. Journal of Health Economics 32 (1): 195–206.

Jaimovich N, Siu H. 2020. Job polarization and jobless recoveries. Review of Economics and Statistics 102 (1): 129–147.

Jargowsky PA. 2014. Segregation, neighborhoods, and schools. In: Lareau A, Goyette, K. (Eds.). Choosing Homes, Choosing Schools: Residential Segregation and the Search for a Good School. (pp. 97–136). Russell Sage Foundation.

Jensen R. 2010. The (perceived) returns to education and the demand for schooling. Quarterly Journal of Economics 125 (2): 515–548.

Jenson R, Miller N. 2017. Keepin' 'Em Down on the Farm: Migration and Strategic Investment in Children's Schooling. National Bureau of Economic Research Working Paper No. 23122. Cambridge, MA: NBER.

Jerch R, Kahn ME, Li S. 2017. The efficiency of local government: The role of privatization and public sector unions. Journal of Public Economics 154 (October): 95–121.

Jerch RL. 2018. The Local Consequences of Federal Mandates: Evidence from the Clean Water Act. Working paper, Johns Hopkins University.

Joassart-Marcelli PM, Musso JA, Wolch JR. 2005. Fiscal consequences of concentrated poverty in a metropolitan region. Annals of the Association of American Geographers 95 (2): 336–356.

Johnson RC. 2019. Children of the dream: Why school integration works. Hachette.

Kain JF. 1968. Housing segregation, negro employment, and metropolitan decentralization. Quarterly Journal of Economics 82 (2): 175–197.

Katz B, Noring L. 2017. The Copenhagen City and Port Development Corporation: A Model for Regenerating Cities. Brookings Institution.

Katz B, Nowak J. 2017. The New Localism: How Cities Can Thrive in the Age of Populism. Brookings Institution.

Kelly J. 2019. JP Morgan reportedly moving thousands of well-paid jobs out of New York City—this does not bode well for workers on Wall Street. Forbes, October 28.

Kiersz A. 2013. The 20 most underrated cities for 20-somethings. Business Insider, October 29.

Kleiman MA. 2009. When Brute Force Fails: How to Have Less Crime and Less Punishment. Princeton University Press.

Kleiman MAR, Saiger AJ. 1990. Drug legalization: The importance of asking the right question. Hofstra Law Review 18 (3): 527–565.

Kleine A. 2019. City on the Line: How Baltimore Transformed Its Budget to Beat the Great Recession and Deliver Outcomes. Rowman and Littlefield.

Kolko J. 2018. The jobs priced out of expensive metros. Indeed Hiring Lab, May 17.

Konrad A. 2019. AOL founder Steve Case launches second $150 million "Rise of the Rest" fund to back entrepreneurs across U.S. Forbes, October 28.

Kramer M. 2019. Turning a vast, post-industrial wilderness into a park in Pittsburgh. Bloomberg CityLab, December 31.

Kreiss D, McGregor SC. 2018. Technology firms shape political communication: The work of Microsoft, Facebook, Twitter, and Google with campaigns during the 2016 US presidential cycle. Political Communication 35 (2): 155–177.

Kristof N. 2019. A better address to change a child's future. New York Times op-ed, August 4.

Krogstad JM. 2019. Key facts about refugees to the U.S. Pew Research Center, October 7.

Krugman P. 1991. History versus expectations. Quarterly Journal of Economics 106 (2): 651–667.

Kuhn M, Schularick M, Steins U. 2018. Income and Wealth Inequality in America, 1949–2016. Federal Reserve Bank of Minneapolis Opportunity and Inclusive Growth Institute Working Paper 9.

Lazear EP. 2001. Educational production. Quarterly Journal of Economics 116 (3): 777–803.

Leibenstein H. 1966. Allocative efficiency vs. "X-efficiency." American Economic Review 56 (3): 392–415.

Levitt SD. 2004. Understanding why crime fell in the 1990s: Four factors that explain the decline and six that do not. Journal of Economic Perspectives 18 (1): 163–190.

Linder C. 2017. Pittsburgh's tech employment grew 12 percent in the last two years, but is that sustainable? Pittsburgh Post-Gazette, July 26.

Loeb P. 2019. After violent weekend, Philly adding new strategies to crime prevention effort. KYW Newsradio, October 21.

Mallach A. 2020. Drilling Down in Baltimore's Neighborhoods: Changes in Racial/Ethnic Composition and Income from 2000 to 2017. Abell Foundation Report.

Manduca R, Sampson RJ. 2019. Punishing and toxic neighborhood environments independently predict the intergenerational social mobility of black and white children. Proceedings of the National Academy of Sciences 116 (16): 7772–7777.

Margo RA. 1992. Explaining the postwar suburbanization of population in the United States: The role of income. Journal of Urban Economics 31 (3): 301–310.

Margolis J. 2018. Detroit welcomes immigrants to spur the city's revival. The World, September 18.

Maryland Department of the Environment. 2019. Childhood Blood Lead Surveillance in Maryland, Annual Report, Appendix A.

Maskin E. 2018. Five reasons ranked-choice voting will improve American democracy. Boston Globe, December 4.

McCabe B. 2012. Changing the game. Johns Hopkins Magazine, Fall.

Meyer T. 2020. Who Wants to Run the Deadliest Big City in America? Politico, May 5.

Michigan Department of Health and Human Services. https://www.michigan.gov/mdhhs/.

Miller M, Seigel B, McComas M, Scrivener L. 2018. Financing Baltimore's Growth: Venture Capital Support for Small Companies. Johns Hopkins 21st Century Cities Initiative.

Milligan C. 2019. High costs put Maryland on a list of the worst states to start a business. Baltimore Business Journal, July 9.

Moffitt R. 2019. The Marginal Labor Supply Disincentives of Welfare Programs. National Bureau of Economic Research Working Paper No. 26028. Cambridge, MA: NBER.

Monroe RG. 2019. It's time to change the narrative on Baltimore. There's a lot worth celebrating. Washington Post, April 26.

Moretti E. 2004. Human capital externalities in cities. In: Handbook of Regional and Urban Economics (Vol. 4, pp. 2243–2291). Elsevier.

Moretti E. 2010 Local multipliers. American Economic Review 100 (2): 373–377.

Moretti E. 2012. The New Geography of Jobs. Houghton Mifflin Harcourt.

National Conference of State Legislatures. 2020. Occupational Licensing Legislation Database.

Neal D. 1995. Industry-specific human capital: Evidence from displaced workers. Journal of Labor Economics 13 (4): 653–677.

Neal D. 1999. The complexity of job mobility among young men. Journal of Labor Economics 17 (2): 237–261.

Neal D, Rick A. 2016. The prison boom and sentencing policy. Journal of Legal Studies 45 (1): 1–41.

Neumark D, Kolko J. 2020. Do enterprise zones create jobs? Evidence from California's enterprise zone program. Journal of Urban Economics 68 (1): 1–9.

Nichols A, Rothstein J. 2016. The earned income tax credit. In: Moffitt R. (Ed.). Economics of Means-Tested Transfer Programs in the United States. Vol 1. University of Chicago Press.

O'Dea J. 2019. St. Louis third for fastest-growing foreign-born population, new census data shows. St. Louis Post-Dispatch, October 10.

Olander L. 2019. The 8 most underrated cities in America. Jetsetter, September 3.

Olsen S. 2014. A house divided—how race colors the path to homeownership. Zillow, January 14.

Open Baltimore. BPD datasets: arrests. Accessed January 2020.

Open Baltimore. BPD employee file as of 10/04/2018. Accessed July 18, 2020.

Opilo E. 2020. Baltimore losing $20 million per month under coronavirus restrictions. Baltimore Sun, April 24.

Oreopoulos P, Von Wachter T, Heisz A. 2012. The short- and long-term career effects of graduating in a recession. American Economic Journal: Applied Economics 4 (1): 1–29.

Owens III R, Rossi-Hansberg E, Sarte PD. 2020. Rethinking Detroit. American Economic Journal: Economic Policy 12 (2): 258–305.

Park RJ, Goodman J, Hurwitz M, Smith J. 2020. Heat and learning. American Economic Journal: Economic Policy 12 (2): 306–309.

Pennsylvania Department of Health. Enterprise Data Dissemination Informatics Exchange. https://www.health.pa.gov/topics/HealthStatistics/EDDIE/Pages/EDDIE.aspx.

Perry A, Rothwell J, Harshbarger D. 2018. The Devaluation of Assets in Black Neighborhoods. Brookings Institution.

Perry A, Rothwell, J, Harshbarger, D. 2020. Five-Star Reviews, One-Star Profits: The Devaluation of Businesses in Black Communities. Brookings Institutution.

Persico C. 2020. Can Pollution Cause Poverty? The Effects of Pollution on Educational, Health and Economic Outcomes. IZA Discussion Paper 12965. IZA Institute of Labor Economics.

Pew Charitable Trusts. 2018. Philadelphia's Immigrants: Who They Are and How They Are Changing the City.

Pietila A. 2010. Not in My Neighborhood: How Bigotry Shaped a Great American City. Ivan R. Dee.

Plank S, DeLuca S, Estacion A. 2008. High school dropout and the role of career and technical education: A survival analysis of surviving high school. Sociology of Education 81 (4): 345–370.

Porter E. 2019. A few cities have cornered innovation jobs. Can that be changed? New York Times, December 9.

Porter E. 2020. A $100 million bet that vacationland can be a tech hub, too. New York Times, January 27.

Porter ME. 1996. An economic strategy for America's inner cities: Addressing the controversy. Review of Black Political Economy 24 (2–3): 303–336.

Poverty and Inequality Research Lab at Johns Hopkins University. 2017. Set-Up City: The Voices of Baltimore Youth after the April 2015 Unrest. 21st Century Cities Initiative.

Raleigh E, Galster G. 2015. Neighborhood disinvestment, abandonment, and crime dynamics. Journal of Urban Affairs 37 (4): 367–396.

Raphael S, Stoll MA. 2001. Can boosting minority car-ownership rates narrow interracial employment gaps? Brookings-Wharton Papers on Urban Affairs, January 1, 99–145.

Reardon SF, Bischoff K. 2016. The Continuing Increase in Income Segregation, 2007–2012. Stanford Center for Education Policy Analysis.

Renn A. 2019. St. Louis blues. City Journal, June 17.

Reyes J. 2007. Environmental Policy as Social Policy? The Impact of Childhood Lead Exposure on Crime. National Bureau of Economic Research Working Paper No. 13097. Cambridge, MA: NBER.

Richman T. 2019. "Not acceptable": Baltimore City Council pushes for action on sewage backups, lagging reimbursement program. Baltimore Sun, November 13.

Richman T. 2019. Baltimore mayor tells agencies to anticipate cuts as city prepares to fund statewide plan to improve schools. Baltimore Sun, November 22.

Riley J. 2019. Teachers unions don't really strike for "the kids." Wall Street Journal op-ed, January 22.

Robb A, Fairlie R. 2007. Why are black-owned businesses less successful than white-owned businesses? The role of families, inheritances, and business human capital. Journal of Labor Economics 25 (2): 289–323.

Rodricks D. 2019. With the help of mentors, these Baltimore squeegee boys are moving into a new business. Baltimore Sun, October 31.

Rodricks D. 2020 In Baltimore, peacemakers fight the violence contagion. Baltimore Sun, February 23.

Roman C, Klein H, Wolff K, Bellamy M, Reeves K. 2017. Philadelphia CeaseFire: Findings from the Impact Evaluation.

Rosenbaum JE, DeLuca S, Miller SR, Roy K. 1999. Pathways into work: Short- and long-term effects of personal and institutional ties. Sociology of Education 72 (July): 179–196.

Rosenthal SS, Ross SL. 2015. Change and persistence in the economic status of neighborhoods and cities. In: Handbook of Regional and Urban Economics (Vol. 5, pp. 1047–1120). Elsevier.

Ross SL. 2011. Social interactions within cities: Neighborhood environments and peer relationships. In: Brooks N, Donaghy K, Knaap G-J (Eds.). The Oxford Handbook of Urban Economics and Planning (pp. 681–704). Oxford University Press.

Rutkow L, McGinty M, Wetter S, Vernick J. 2019. Local public health policymakers' views on state preemption: Results of a national survey, 2018. American Journal of Public Health 109 (8): 1107–1110.

Sachs JD. 2012. From millennium development goals to sustainable development goals. The Lancet 379 (9832): 2206–2211.

Saiz A. 2010. The geographic determinants of housing supply. Quarterly Journal of Economics 125 (3): 1253–1296.

Schelling TC. 1972. A process of residential segregation: neighborhood tipping. In: Pascal AH (Ed.). Racial Discrimination in Economic Life. Lexington Books.

Sharkey P, Torrats-Espinosa G, Takyar D. 2017. Community and the crime decline: The causal effect of local nonprofits on violent crime. American Sociological Review 82 (6): 1214–1240.

Sigman H. 1998. Liability funding and superfund clean-up remedies. Journal of Environmental Economics and Management 35 (3): 205–224.

Sigman H. 2010. Environmental liability and redevelopment of old industrial land. Journal of Law and Economics 53 (2): 289–306.

Slattery C, Zidar O. 2020. Evaluating State and Local Business Tax Incentives. National Bureau of Economic Research Working Paper No. 26603. Cambridge, MA: NBER.

Stein M, Grigg J, Cronister C, Chavis C, Connolly F. 2017. Getting to High School in Baltimore: Student Commuting and Public Transportation. Baltimore Education Research Consortium.

Stoll M, Raphael S, Holzer H. 2004. Black job applicants and the hiring officer's race. Industrial and Labor Relations Review 57 (2), https://doi.org/10.1177/001979390405700206.

Strauss V. 2019. Why school integration works. Washington Post, May 16.

Tach L, Edin K. 2011. The relationship contexts of young disadvantaged men. Annals of the American Academy of Political and Social Science 635 (1): 76–94.

Taylor J. 2018. An Analysis of Low-Skill Occupations in Philadelphia. Economy League of Greater Philadelphia.

Topel RH, Ward MP. 1992. Job mobility and the careers of young men. Quarterly Journal of Economics 107 (2): 439–479.

Troesken W. 2004. Water, Race, and Disease. MIT Press.

Turney K, Clampet-Lundquist S, Edin K, Kling J, Duncan G. 2006. Neighborhood effects on barriers to employment: Results from a randomized housing mobility experiment in Baltimore. Brookings-Wharton Papers on Urban Affairs, 2006, 137–187.

Uhlig H. 2006. Regional labor markets, network externalities and migration: The case of German reunification. American Economic Review 96 (2): 383–387.

Uhlig H. 2008. The slow decline of East Germany. Journal of Comparative Economics 36 (4): 517–541.

Urban Institute. Explore Your School's Changing Demographics. Accessed February 2020. https://www.urban.org/features/explore-your-schools-changing-demographics.

US Census Bureau. USA Counties: File Layout. https://www.census.gov/library/publications/2011/compendia/usa-counties-2011/file-layout.html.

US Department of Transportation Maritime Administration. U.S. Waterborne Foreign Container Trade by U.S. Customs Ports, 2000–2017.

US Department of Housing and Urban Development. 2011. The Poplar Nehemiah Homeownership Development. Content archived April 20.

Vishwanath A. 2018. St. Louis in focus: "Little Bosnia." Student Life, November 28.

Waite LJ, Gallagher M. 2001. The Case for Marriage: Why Married People Are Happier, Healthier, and Better Off Financially. Broadway Books.

Waldfogel J. 2008. The median voter and the median consumer: Local private goods and population composition. Journal of Urban Economics 63 (2): 567–582.

Warnock D. 2015. Baltimore voters should choose school board members. Baltimore Sun, March 18.

Watson A. 2020. "The strategy is working": Milwaukee's crime rate steadily decreasing. Wisconsin Public Radio, January 14.

Webster D, Buggs, S, Crifasi, C. 2018. Estimating the Effects of Law Enforcement and Public Health Interventions Intended to Reduce Gun Violence in Baltimore. Johns Hopkins Center for Gun Policy and Research.

Wenger, Y. 2020. At what cost? For Baltimore's poorest families, the child support system exacts a heavy price—and it's hurting whole communities. Baltimore Sun, March 5.

Wheeler TB, Cox, E. 2013. Harbor Point project stirs environmental concerns. Baltimore Sun, August 31.

WHYY. 2012. EPA approves Philly's $2 billion green stormwater plan. WHYY radio, April 11.

Wilen H. 2018. Maryland and Baltimore improve in small business friendliness rankings. Baltimore Business Journal, August 14.

Willms JD. 2000. School Choice and Community Segregation: Findings from Scotland. In Kerckhoff A (Ed.). Generating Social Stratification: Toward a New Research Agenda. Routledge.

Wilson WJ. 2008. The political and economic forces shaping concentrated poverty. Political Science Quarterly 123 (4): 555–571.

Wilson WJ. 2012. The Truly Disadvantaged: The Inner City, the Underclass, and Public Policy. University of Chicago Press.

Wood P. 2019. How much in taxes could Maryland make off legal weed? It's hard to say. Baltimore Sun, August 19.

Zumer B. 2019. Opponents criticize plan for "forced Section 8" in Baltimore County. Fox 45 News, October 28.

Zurawik D. 2018. Mayor's call to "change the narrative" is not the answer to Baltimore's perception problems. Baltimore Sun, January 4.

Index